First Line Supervision

2d Edition

Robert T. Thetford

Louis M. Harris, Jr.

Institute for Criminal Justice, Inc., Montgomery, Alabama

© 2002 – 2010 by Institute for Criminal Justice Education, Inc.

All rights reserved. No part of this book may be reproduced, stored in a retrieval system or transmitted in any form or by any means – electronic, electrostatic, magnetic tape, mechanical, photocopying, recording, or otherwise – without permission in writing from the Institute for Criminal Justice Education, Inc. (ICJE), P.O. Box 293, Montgomery, Alabama 36101.

This publication is designed to provide accurate and authoritative information in regard to the subject matter covered. It is sold with the understanding that the publisher is not engaged in rendering legal, accounting, or other professional services. If legal advice or other expert assistance is required, the services of a competent professional person should be sought.

All references to gender within this book have been made with consideration to consistency.

For information on all publications available from ICJE, visit ICJE online at www.icje.org or telephone 334/280-0020, fax 334/281-4367.

Printed in the United States of America.

ISBN: 1453811729

EAN-13: 9781453811726

TABLE OF CONTENTS

About the Authors…………………………………………………………	iv
Preface………………………………………………………………………..	v
Acknowledgements…………………………………………………………	v
CHAPTER 1: Introduction to First Line Supervision……………………	1
CHAPTER 2: Leadership Basics…………………………………………	4
CHAPTER 3: Leadership Ethics…………………………………………	30
CHAPTER 4: Goal Setting…….…………………………………………..	42
CHAPTER 5: Time Management………………………………………..	49
CHAPTER 6: Motivation………………………………………………...	64
CHAPTER 7: Communication…………………………………………..	73
CHAPTER 8: Problem Solving…………………………………………..	82
CHAPTER 9: Budgeting………………………………………………….	100
CHAPTER 10: Stress Management……………………………………...	109
CHAPTER 11: Conflict Resolution……………………………………...	119
CHAPTER 12: Practical Negotiation…………………………………….	126
CHAPTER 13: Supervisory Liability……………………………………	136
CHAPTER 14: Meeting Strategies and Networking……………………..	154
CHAPTER 15: Media Relations…………………………………………	161
CHAPTER 16: The Future……………………………………………….	169

About the Authors

Robert T. Thetford, J.D., is a practicing attorney in Montgomery, Alabama where he specializes in mediation procedures and consulting for police agencies and private industry. He is also an adjunct professor of criminal justice at Faulkner University, teaching a variety of legal courses along with terrorism and Web-based investigations. In 1998 he co-founded the Institute for Criminal Justice Education, Inc., a nonprofit organization for which he is the managing director. He is a graduate of The University of Alabama Law School.

Dr. Thetford has over 25 years' experience as a prosecutor, Special Agent and Division Legal Counsel with the FBI. A native of Montgomery, Alabama, and a member of the Alabama Bar, he has provided legal advice and instruction to a wide variety of agencies. In addition to investigating political corruption, white-collar crime and terrorism cases, he worked as a Certified Police Instructor, Legal Instructor, Government Mediator, and was a Relief Supervisor for over ten years. Awards received during his last assignment in Alabama included selection as Federal Law Enforcement Officer of the Year (Middle District of Alabama) and a Director's Commendation with Presidential Recognition for coordination of the investigation into the murder of a Federal Judge.

Robert Thetford may be contacted at P.O. Box 293, Montgomery, AL 36101, Tel 334/280-0020, E-mail address rthetford@icje.org.

Louis M. Harris, Jr., D.P.A., is a professor of Criminal Justice and Chair of the Criminal Justice and Legal Studies Department at Faulkner University in Montgomery, Alabama. Prior to Faulkner University he served as an FBI agent for 25 years with investigative duty assignments in Oregon, Washington and Alabama. He served as a relief supervisor in Seattle, Washington and senior resident agent on the Yakima Indian Reservation. He received a Master of Science degree in Criminal Justice from Troy State University and Doctor of Public Administration from The University of Alabama.

Dr. Harris served as Chief of the Campus Security Department at Faulkner University for almost three years. He has written a number of articles on law enforcement and management-related topics and co-authored three books; Informant Development, First Line Supervision, and Instructor Development. He has served on the Crime Stoppers Board of Directors, East Montgomery Historical Society, and is currently serving on the Alabama Sentencing Commission. He is a ministry leader at his church and annually teaches an adult Bible study class.

Dr. Harris may be contacted at Faulkner University, 5345 Atlanta Hwy, Montgomery, AL 36109, Tel/ 334/386-7188, E-mail address lharris@faulkner.edu.

Preface

First Line Supervision continues to be a work in progress. This book began in 1998 as the authors' handouts and notes in a management course taught at a law enforcement academy in Alabama. The course began as 24 hours of instruction which has been extended to a 30-hour course over a five-day period. This book was adopted as a college course text in 2001 and has introduced hundreds of students to the basics of first line supervision. Initially, the authors taught this course in an academic and training setting, receiving feedback from criminal justice professionals and graduated students who entered the field and related their experiences. However, the demand for multiple classes each year led the authors to recruiting additional instructors. Those instructors also provided feedback which appears in this edition of *First Line Supervision*.

The authors present a text that is intended for active use by students during each class session. Spaces are provided for note taking and jotting down individual reactions to questions posed by the authors. Group discussion questions, self tests and questions to ponder individually are presented to challenge student interaction and thought. The authors assume that students using this text have some experience or exposure to the criminal justice system, and as such, bring a wealth of knowledge and experience to the classroom. Student discussions provide students with an opportunity to share personal experiences and significantly contribute to the substance of the text.

The second edition contains additional concepts and practices offered by students, instructors and criminal justice practitioners. A chapter on Media Relations was added to recognize the expanded role first line supervisors play in departmental communications. Comments are encouraged and feedback from students will ensure that the next edition of this text continues to provide a much-needed resource for first line supervisors.

Acknowledgements

The authors continue to express appreciation to their families who suffered and endured with them over the past eight years as the course was taught and management ideas were discussed over the dinner table. We also acknowledge the many criminal justice professionals who shared their personal stories of management experiences and provided further insight into the unique challenges faced by 21st century supervisors. And finally, but most importantly, the authors acknowledge their Creator who gave us the ability and opportunity to complete this task.

Introduction   Chapter 1

If your actions inspire others to dream more, learn more, do more and become more, you are a leader. John Quincy Adams

This course is designed to present the basic concepts and techniques of supervising in a criminal justice environment, while also providing an overview of leadership skills necessary to prepare criminal justice practitioners to meet the challenges of the 21st century.

This book is written for those practicing supervisors who wish to review and update their knowledge of basic management and leadership principles or for those who aspire to be supervisors in the future. While written from a criminal justice perspective, the principles contained in this work apply equally to any workplace environment, in private enterprise as well as the public sector.

The authors understand that not all of the material presented will be equally applicable to each person; however, every reader should discover some new principles in each section which, if applied to the workplace environment, should improve skills and job performance to a significant degree.

Similarly, the skills learned here are transferable to virtually all situations, whether they are at work, at home, or outside activities such as charitable or recreational pursuits. Just as in most other educational efforts, the skills learned depend not as much on the ability or experience of the student as on the willingness and determination of the student to learn and to apply what he or she has learned.

With these ideas in mind, let us examine the following principles:

Habit

Merriam-Webster's Collegiate Dictionary defines habit as "an acquired mode of behavior that has become nearly or completely involuntary." It is generally accepted that if a person follows the same behavior pattern for 21 to 25 consecutive days, the behavior pattern will be adopted as a habit.

The principles in this book did not originate with the authors. They have been obtained from various sources, including personal observation, educational courses and a number of texts. It is the opinion of the authors, however, that the ideas and suggestions here, if studied and adopted as personal behavior patterns habits, will measurably enhance professional and personal skills, and may result in increased opportunities for advancement.

The Pareto Principle

Vilfredo Pareto was a 19th Century Italian economist and sociologist who discovered that 80 percent of the output of any given endeavor was produced by approximately 20 percent of the input. This has subsequently become known as the Pareto Principle or simply the 80/20 Rule.

The Rule can apply to more than the pure input/output ratio, however, and somehow is accurate in a number of applications, including:

- Addressing the most troublesome 20 percent of a problem will solve 80 percent of it.
- Within any organization, 20 percent of the individuals will cause 80 percent of the organizational problems.
- In public involvement, 20 percent of the people will command 80 percent of your time.
- Within any given organization, 80 percent of the work is done by 20 percent of the employees.
- In most law enforcement investigative organizations, 80 percent of the productive cases are developed and managed by 20 percent of the investigative personnel.

Keep the Pareto principle in mind as you read through the chapters of this book. Look for ways in which the principle may be applied in the situations presented and also in your own experiences. You may be surprised to find that it can be applied accurately in many unusual cases.

Change and How We Cope With It

A second theme predominantly found throughout this book is the inevitability of change in the workplace and the necessity of organizational leadership to adapt to it. This work examines various reactive responses by supervisors to cultural change and offers suggested supervisory approaches which may be more effective in preparing employees to meet the challenges of the current workplace environment.

Think about the answers to the following questions:

- How has our society changed over the past 20 to 30 years?

- How have crimes and criminals changed?

- How has law enforcement changed?

- What skills do managers need today?

- What new skills will managers need five years from now?

A changing environment demands that supervisors constantly evaluate their management style against existing conditions, while they must also continuously upgrade their knowledge, skills and techniques. Today's supervisor, especially in criminal justice, will find that there are limited opportunities for official training, and yet training must be held if the supervisor is to survive in or advance beyond the first line position.

Because of the need for skills improvement, many management experts believe that supervisors should spend at least three percent of their income on books, tapes, films and courses designed to make them more proficient in their careers.

Like it or not, the burden of maintaining and improving competence rests squarely on the employee, not on the department. Studying this book and applying the principles is a step, but only a first step, in preparing for your future.

Leadership Basics   Chapter 2

God grant that men of principle shall be our principal men. Thomas Jefferson

This study is directed toward individuals who either currently occupy a first-line supervisory position or who desire to occupy a supervisory position in the future. A first-line supervisor is a term describing any entry-level to mid-level supervisor who is not in a policymaking position (policy decisions are those which define the fundamental structure of achieving the mission of an organization). An individual who is engaged in making policy decisions for an organization is generally considered to be in a management position above the first-line supervisory level.

Perceptions

People often think of a supervisor as a person in total control over an organizational unit, whose word is law and who enjoys perks commensurate with the responsibility of a supervisor. Perhaps this perception was, in fact, reality at some time in the past but it is certainly no longer true in today's workplace environment. Just why is it that past methods fail to work in the employment culture of today?

According to futurist and author Alvin Toffler, there were three distinct stages in the historical evolution of technology. The first was the Agricultural Age, which lasted from the time of Adam to about 1745 in the United States. This stage was characterized by subsistence agriculture and saw few innovative changes in technology. The second stage was the industrial age, which lasted from 1745 to 1955, and witnessed progressive changes such as the steam engine, telegraph, telephone, radio and electric power. The third stage, described by Toffler as the Information Age, began in 1955, the year in which white-collar employees first outnumbered blue collar workers in the United States. Perhaps the most accurate one word description for the Information Age would be change.

Today, change permeates the culture of every advanced nation and certainly affects every aspect of American life, including the workplace. Change has been accelerated through both external and internal factors. As new technologies have become available they have been rapidly assimilated and embraced by society because of the nature of technology to enhance lifestyles and increase productivity. We now face a bewildering array in choices of competing technologies both in the workplace and the home, all of which promise to make life better or more productive.

At the same time, internal factors have changed in the sense that young workers often seem to be guided by a different moral compass from that which guided their forefathers. The MTV generation has certainly heard the media message of *carpe diem,* the existential belief that one should live only for the moment, and this theme is certainly played repeatedly in their lack of long-term commitment to family, profession or employer. This lack of long-term commitment is evidenced by the increased number of career employment changes expected for today's employee (10.3) as compared to five or less for an employee entering the job market in the 1960s. A booming economy and increased availability of employment opportunity certainly account for some of the increase in job changing. But a generalized lack of commitment toward any profession or employer along with the perception that employers owe no job security to their employees have certainly contributed to the frequent career changes observed today.

Response to a changing environment often determines success or failure in both the business world and criminal justice related professions. An examination of the changes occurring over the last 10 years in law-enforcement reflects a response to a changing criminal environment as well as the embracing of new technologies to manage criminal justice data, some of which were not even available to law-enforcement a decade ago.

Computers have drastically altered workplace methodology in criminal justice and continue to play an ever-increasing role throughout the field. Computers have made available the implementation of such systems as:

- Community Policing Techniques

- NCIC 2000

- AFIS Fingerprint System

- Vehicle Computers

- GIS Imaging Databases

- Major Case Databases

- DVP Radios

- Fax Machines

- Pagers

- Cellular telephones

- Internet (e-mail) and Intranet Communications

At the same time, crime and the criminals who commit crimes have changed. As new weapon technologies have become available, criminals have become more sophisticated and often more violent. Cracking, a crime unheard of a few short years ago, has become commonplace along with identity theft, credit card billing theft, cyber-espionage and exotic crimes such as bitnapping, Denial of Service attacks and cyber-extortion. In the past, fewer than 10 percent of all criminals used computers. It was estimated that today, 90 percent of all criminals in the United States will be computer literate.

The workplace environment has changed as rapidly as the culture and this is reflected in today's workplace diversity, even in law-enforcement. In Alabama, almost 10 percent of the state's police officers are women. Twenty years ago this figure was less than one percent. Twenty-five years ago the FBI had only three black Special Agents. Today there are 640. There are over 1,700 female Special Agents with the FBI today, while in 1971 there were none.

In order to adequately respond to the demands produced by an constantly changing workplace environment, it is necessary for today's supervisor to stay current in his or her field. The ability to remain current in one's chosen field often separates those who are selected for senior management positions from those who remain in first-line supervisory positions throughout their careers. It has been suggested that a supervisor or aspiring supervisor should spend at least three percent of his or her income on books, tapes, films and courses designed to enhance the supervisor's professional ability.

This education may be formal as in a college or master's degree program, or it may be obtained informally through professional training programs.

Leadership

So just what is a leader and how should he or she function? A leader has three basic characteristics that have been described like three legs of a stool. These three legs or characteristics are ambition, expertise and integrity.

If any of these characteristics is missing, there will be a severe problem with the leadership ability of the individual. For example, having integrity and expertise but no ambition describes a person who is competent and a may even be well liked, but who will do nothing to drive the organization forward. Having ambition and integrity but no expertise guarantees that the organization will fail for lack of competent direction, and a person who has both ambition and expertise but is lacking in integrity will quickly develop into a dictator or tyrant.

Management

Management has been described as the process of accomplishing the goals of the organization through others. Managers are involved in carrying out four distinct functions for the organization:

- Planning: defining what is going to be done; setting objectives.

- Organizing: collecting resources and placing them so they can work together.

- Directing: insuring that the resources are applied to the planned tasks on time.

- Controlling: making sure the objectives continue to be met and the mission is accomplished.

Basic Skills

There are certain basic skills that managers need to possess. They may be categorized into technical skills and human relation skills. Technical skills include applied skills such as firearms proficiency, computer skills and the understanding of departmental policy, criminal laws and criminal procedure. Technical administrative skills would include planning, organizing, directing and controlling. In addition to technical skills, a supervisor must also possess certain human relation skills such as communication and motivation techniques, persuasion abilities, and even conceptual skills such as analytical thinking and some forward vision.

Leadership Definitions

Leadership is the art of influencing others to follow your direction in attaining the department's objectives. How does this differ from the definition of management? It has been called an art rather than a science, why?

The key to leadership is influencing other people. Note here that leadership does not necessarily involve using force or deliberately imposing a person's will on others. Although force may be a necessary part of leadership under certain conditions, such as in military combat, the ability to influence others short of using force or threats is characteristic of a leader. There is no set formula for this that works in every situation, and the ability to influence often depends upon the environment, the personality of the leader and the group dynamics present during a given situation.

A leader must assume several roles in order to be effective. These roles include being an **advocate** (for both the employees and the department), an **educator, referee, coach, counselor** and, when the occasion dictates, a **disciplinarian.**

Primary leadership traits include **knowledge, enthusiasm, dedication, persistence, dependability, self-confidence, maturity and drive**. Additional leadership traits include **intelligence, discernment, judgment and formal education**.

Leadership Styles

There are two basic styles of leadership as described by Douglas McGregor. The first style, entitled **Theory X, is an authoritarian style** which assumes that although employees may be skilled in their jobs, they are basically lazy, dislike work and must be told what to do. This theory further assumes that given an opportunity to do so, employees will naturally attempt to avoid responsibility and so the organizational goals will not be reached without close supervision.

The exact opposite of this view is entitled **Theory Y, a democratic style** of leadership which assumes that competent employees are intelligent, that they not only want to work but want to do well at their jobs and often can and do contribute ideas which augment the efficiency of the workplace.

There is a third style that, although given somewhat facetiously, accurately describes the style of some managers. The official title for the style is Free Reign, but it is also known as **Theory 0 (Theory Ostrich)** because the manager sometimes is viewed as having his or her head in the sand, thus providing no real leadership or guidance at all.

Managerial Grid

```
Employee Oriented
(1-9) 9                                              (9-9) 9
      8                                      8
      7                              7
      6                      6
              (5-5)
      5              5
      4      4
      3  3
      2 2
(1-1) 1  2  3  4  5  6  7  8  (9-1) 9
                  Task Oriented
```

Viewing a leadership style from the perspective of whether or not it is Task Oriented vs. Employee Oriented can be depicted graphically using The Managerial Grid developed by Blake and Molten. A purely **Task Oriented leader is primarily concerned with**

production, efficiency and timely completion of the assigned project, while an Employee Oriented leader is more concerned with human needs.

Managerial Grid

Utilizing the Grid, a 9-1 leader is totally Task Oriented while a 1-9 leader is totally Employee Oriented. What about a 1-1 leader or a 1-5 leader? A 9-9 leader has a strong concern for both task and employee interests. In other words, a 9-9 leader as interested in both employee interest and production. This leader's attitude is that our unit will do the job correctly and that we will be good to our people while they are doing the job.

While it seems that a 9-9 leader would present the best of both worlds in all situations, in actuality a true leader should be flexible enough to be a 1-9 leader or a 9-1 leader when the situation warrants. For example, during emergencies when timing is critical, a 9-1 response is appropriate, but when an employee has a serious personal problem, 1-9 approach may be best. Leaders must understand than a 9-1 or a 1-9 approach are both considered only applicable in the short term while a 9-9 approach is best overall. In your experience, where do most supervisors fall on the grid?

Contingency Model

The Contingency Model of leadership, developed by Fred E. Fiedler, takes the Managerial Grid and applies it to various situations or contingencies to arrive at a particular and appropriate leadership style. Fiedler first examines the **leader-subordinate relations** of the employment situation. The first question addressed is whether or not labor-management relations are considered good or poor. In other words, do first line officers or employees work well with the organizational management?

Next, the **task structure** is analyzed with the determining factor being the amount of freedom an employee is given to do a particular job. A highly structured task will give little discretion to the employee in carrying out various tasks. Examples of a highly structured task would include production line work, fast food handling or police dispatcher duties. Unstructured work plays a great deal of discretion to the employee in carrying out various tasks and would include research and some investigative work.

Finally, **leadership position power** is examined by determining the amount of power given to the leader by the organizational structure. To do this, the structure must be analyzed to determine whether or not management will strongly back the supervisor's authority in his/her relations with the employees. A secondary analysis determines how much authority the employees have been given to challenge the leader by appealing unpopular decisions to the leader's supervisor. Thus, the leader's position power will be characterized as either weak or strong.

Contingency Model

Leader-Subordinate Relations	Task Structure	Leader Position Power	Appropriate Leadership Style
Good	Structured	Strong	Task Oriented
Good	Structured	Weak	Task Oriented
Good	Unstructured	Strong	Somewhat Task Oriented
Good	Unstructured	Weak	People Oriented
Poor	Structured	Strong	People Oriented
Poor	Structured	Weak	Somewhat People Oriented
Poor	Unstructured	Strong	Somewhat Task Oriented
Poor	Unstructured	Weak	Task Oriented

Leadership vs. Management

So just what is the difference between a leader and a manager? Is there really a difference between the two, or is this just a question of semantics? People in private industry and government often interchange the two as having the same essence; when in fact, they have dramatically different definitions. In general, an employee is thought to work for a manager and with a leader. A manager tends to think of employees and in terms of costs and benefits. The leader, however, tends to think of employees as a valuable resource base upon which the leader can draw support. As Stephen Covey puts it, a manager thinks in terms of doing things right while a leader thinks in terms of doing the right things.

In his book, *The Unheavenly City*, Edward Banfield described the world as being divided into two classes of persons, the upper class and the lower class. Banfield believes that the major difference between the two is shown in their vision of the future and how they act upon this vision. Upper class people tend to think in future terms and are willing to forego present gratification for future gain. On the other hand, lower class people, having no ability to think or act in future terms, are more likely to seek instant gratification on a daily basis and to deny themselves nothing despite an inability to pay for the object of their desire. According to Banfield, the class to which one belongs depends not upon race, sex or national origin. It also does not depend upon wealth or material accumulation; therefore, an individual of meager means and little material accumulation with a future vision may be considered upper class, while an individual of considerable material wealth who lacks a future vision would be considered lower class.

Because of their future vision, supervisor/leaders would invariably be numbered in the ranks of the upper class. They are characterized by not being afraid to try new approaches and often encourage innovation even with the understanding that failure will inevitably accompany many attempts to innovate. Failing at particular projects is not, however, the same as failing as an organization. Failing organizations often fail because they are over-managed and under-led. During his employment at Ford Motor Company, Lee Iacocca frequently promoted his idea for a new type of vehicle. His ideas were constantly rebuffed and it was not until he later transferred to Chrysler that his idea met with some acceptance. The result was one of the greatest success stories in automotive history, the minivan.

Is it possible, then, to make a leader out of anyone? While there is such a thing as a "natural leader," it is simply not possible to make leaders of anyone. That being said, leadership traits can be taught to all those who understand future vision and demonstrate an aptitude toward applying that vision to the workplace environment.

In applying the vision a leader quickly understands that his or her power to produce depends not upon force or threats but upon influence. The leader may possess organizational power (the power to reward or punish) which accompanies the leadership position, but this power alone is generally not considered sufficient for maximum production. A supervisor may only expect the best, sustained work from employees when the supervisor's organizational power is accompanied by personal power (charismatic power) that must be earned on a continuing basis by the aspiring leader.

Leadership Traits

The first trait of a true leader is a **willingness to serve** and support the employees. This is certainly not a new innovation but was outlined by Jesus in Matthew Chapter 20, Verse 27: *"**And whosoever will be chief among you, let him be your servant**."* This is the opposite of arrogance, which often manifests itself in the attitude of, "my way or the highway."

A second leadership trait involves **giving credit to one's employees** rather than taking credit for any job well done. This acknowledges the major contributions by the team members and has the added benefit of building loyalty rapidly. The flip side to this leadership trait involves taking personal responsibility for any failures instead of assigning blame to the employees individually or as a group.

The ability to listen and discern are rare but learnable traits which should be employed by every leader. Many managers listen only to what they want to hear and filter out much of what is actually being said to them. A true leader not only listens but listens well. The discerning supervisor understands the difference between positions (what a person says) and interests (what a person really means) and acts accordingly. A leader listens to problems with the perspective of encouraging employees not only to present problems but also to propose solutions. Listening skills are so important that entire training courses have been designed to develop these skills.

A fourth basic leadership trait involves **the use of humor**, especially the ability of a supervisor to laugh at himself or herself. Those who are unable to do so demonstrate a decided lack of confidence in their own abilities or in their position. The ability and willingness to laugh at one's own expense characterizes a person who is confident in his or her own abilities and who is not afraid to show a vulnerable, human side when the situation calls for it. This implies a corollary aspect of leadership: that of knowing one's strengths and weaknesses and playing to strengths while attempting to eliminate or work around weaknesses.

Every would-be leader should have a **mentor or coach** and every true leader should mentor or coach those showing potential for leadership. The best organizational structures provide for a mentoring program either on an official basis or unofficial basis. Mentors are distinguished from departmental training officers in that they actually help a person's career changes and decisions over a period of time. Mentors do not always act out of a true sense of altruism because they are aware that at some point in their own careers, there exists the possibility that the person who is being mentored may eventually be in a position to help them. Despite the motive involved, the mentoring system works well in most organizational structures and should be encouraged by policymakers. Many organizations promote mentoring outside of the normal chain of command, reasoning that the best advice for an employee would be given by a person who was not directly involved in the employee's performance appraisal or direct chain of command.

Mentoring, especially within a formal organizational structure, involves training an employee to take the place of a leader. Many supervisors feel extremely threatened by the thought of training someone to take their place and consequently they refuse to do so. While this reluctance is natural and understandable, it often creates a situation in which the supervisor will be ineligible for promotion simply because there is no one available with the skills necessary to replace the supervisor after he or she is promoted into another position.

Other traits include **fairness and toughness**. Fairness includes the perception that all employees are treated equally according to the situation at hand. Of course, all employees are not equal and therefore have no reasonable expectation of being treated equally in every situation. Employees with differing abilities and experience levels should be treated in accordance with their abilities and experience.
A leader must also be able to make tough decisions when the situation calls for it. To be perceived as weak and indecisive in a situation which calls for action will quickly cause a supervisor to lose both respect and effectiveness. General George S. Patton believed that decisiveness as a leadership quality was absolutely necessary: "We herd sheep, we drive cattle, we lead people. Lead me, follow me, or get out of my way."

Being tough and fair are balanced by having **a protective attitude** toward those who are supervised. In the 1980s, a newly promoted law enforcement supervisor was advised by his boss to keep the boss informed about any problems encountered, including personnel problems (he was to supervise employees at a remote location). The supervisor answered by saying, "Boss, you will only hear about problems if I can't handle them." This demonstrated confidence in the supervisor's ability to handle both the job and the employees correctly, and also telegraphed to his boss the supervisor's desire to be protective of his employees.

A final character trait shared by true leaders is **a strong sense of ethics and duty**. Throughout history, people have been drawn to and naturally follow a leader who exhibits high moral character. Leaders who are both competent and ethical inspire trust and loyalty from their subordinates. The trust and loyalty, if reciprocated, frequently result in extraordinary production and accomplishment.

Leadership Development

Often, at the initial stage of a supervisor's career, there is a pronounced lack of the self-confidence which can only be gained through experience. It is at this stage that a leader must begin to exude self-confidence, even though he or she may be unsure that the decisions being made are always correct. The aspiring leader must understand that self-confidence is derived from accomplishment, and accomplishment from experience. Experience will also produce the self-realization of the leader's various strengths and weaknesses. Strong leaders consistently play to their strengths and strive to eliminate their weaknesses. One way of determining strengths and weaknesses is through the construction of systems that provide reflective feedback. Trusted advisers who are not "yes men /women," but who will provide honest appraisals and constructive criticism when asked are literally worth their weight in gold to a leader, and can attribute greatly to the leader's success.

Another means of obtaining feedback and advice is through the implementation of a mentoring system. Most large organizations have either a formal or informal mentoring structure, and many high-ranking administrators attribute their advancement to their mentors. Some leadership experts believe that mentors should not be directly in the chain of command in order to preclude any conflict of interest. They also feel that a mentor outside of the direct chain of command is in the best position to assist the person mentored through indirect influence. Mentors, or coaches as they sometimes are called, are necessary in a large organization and are very helpful even in a small department. In the final analysis, however, one must take personal responsibility for learning the art of leadership despite the existence of mentors, training programs and (hopefully) a terrific staff. The best leadership school in the world will not turn an individual into a leader if the individual lacks the incentive to learn and apply the principles observed. The authors have trained hundreds of first line law enforcement and corrections officers in leadership fundamentals over the past few years and this fact has repeatedly been proved true. Conversely, however, even a mediocre leader can dramatically improve his or her leadership ability through initiative and the application of basic leadership principles.

New Supervisors

The first few months can be extremely rough on a new supervisor. Reactions from the supervised employees can vary from jealousy (thinking that they should have been chosen) to playing up to the new supervisor. Some employees enjoy "testing" a new supervisor immediately, and occasionally employees will even attempt to undermine a supervisor's authority, but most will adopt a "wait and see" attitude for the first few weeks or so.

The first and most important decision made by new supervisor upon assuming the job is to make no immediate changes unless specifically instructed to do so. This also holds true for even experienced supervisors upon assuming a new management position. The key here is to take the position with humility.

The new supervisor should immediately review the personnel files of the employees and have an initial interview with each. During this interview the supervisor should essentially get to know the employee, including his or her ambitions, evaluations of the employee's own competency and the employee's perspective about what is going well and not so well with the organization. The supervisor should reassure each employee that it is the supervisor's role is to assist the employees in doing their jobs, not to do the job for them.

Supervising Friends

It is especially difficult for a newly appointed supervisor when the employees consider themselves close friends of the new supervisor. In this situation, many employees will expect preferential treatment while others will be jealous and will challenge the supervisor's authority. They may act as though they are colleagues rather than employees and may quickly trade on past relationships. In some cases supervisors tend to overcompensate and demand more from friends they supervise than from others. Supervisors placed in this position should readily acknowledge both their own discomfort and the discomfort of their employees. At the same time, however, they should emphasize the fact that the supervisor and the employees are a team and that they must work together to accomplish the goals of the organization.

Supervising Older People or More Experienced People

In large organizational structures, the policy of promoting those (often younger employees) who show management aptitude and blend into the "organizational mold" rather than promoting individuals who have demonstrated actual leadership in the field has often produced significant and endemic problems because of the lack of real leadership and experience in the ranks of first line supervisors. As time passes, this will inevitably result in lowering the competence level of the managerial pool and will ultimately produce policy makers who are strictly managers with little to no real leadership skills.

Because they are often younger than the people they supervise, **many new supervisors find it very difficult to supervise older or more experienced employees.** This is often the case with supervisors who are not comfortable with their own leadership abilities or who are easily intimidated by those thought to be "experts" in their fields.

Older employees who are not in supervisory positions frequently will not apply for the position themselves but resent others, especially younger employees, occupying any position of authority over them. Still others are aware that they are not eligible for the position themselves but are envious of those who occupy the position.

Employees frequently will act toward new supervisors as if the employees are experts in the field while the supervisor is shown to have little or no technical knowledge. They may also bristle at suggestions, stating that the requested activity had been attempted before and had not solved the problem.

Another tactic will be to withhold information from the supervisor in an attempt to make the supervisor performed poorly.

The above examples all point to a demonstrated lack of respect for the supervisor's authority and must be met head-on or the supervisor will experience a less than satisfactory existence in this position. Supervisors must understand that what is essential for leadership is not being liked, but being respected. Being liked is not necessary and sometimes will actually hinder operations. On the other hand, having the respect of one's employees will result in employees giving their best effort.

Because respect must be earned, and because older employees are extremely resistant to change, new supervisors must exercise extreme caution not to make unnecessary modifications to the workplace environment immediately upon assuming command.

New supervisors should recognize that many employees have much more experience at their jobs than they have and therefore they must not try to bluff their competence level. It is often helpful for the supervisor to even admit that he or she does not have all of the answers and will be relying on the employees for guidance. This immediately places the employees at ease and demonstrates that the supervisor is interested in a team approach and is not going to impose his or her will as a substitute for experience or good judgment. There is also no prohibition against the supervisor asking for help or for suggestions about how to handle given situations or solve specific problems. An experienced leader will frequently seek options, acknowledging that there is wisdom in the counsel of wise subordinates. The very worst situation occurs when a supervisor refuses to adopt a course of action simply because the idea did not originate with the supervisor. This is a frequent occurrence with new supervisors who are unsure of their authority and competence.

Admitting that the supervisor does not have a monopoly on wisdom is the first step toward team building and efficiency in accomplishing organizational goals. Bottom Line: Failing to ask for help can greatly imperil a supervisor's position. Using employees as a sounding board not only allows the supervisor to see things from a different perspective, it quickly builds self-worth for the employees and respect for the supervisor.

Supervising Inexperienced Employees

Today's supervisors, whether experienced or inexperienced, are greatly challenged when supervising younger, less experienced people. **Younger employees tend not to be as serious about work as older generations and change jobs with much more frequency**. They generally have less actual worldly knowledge (except for video games and computer literacy) than prior generations although they may possess a more advanced formal educational level. Because of their lack of knowledge and dedication, as a general rule younger workers require closer supervision for a longer period of time than their predecessors.

Because of the expense involved in hiring, training, and retaining good employees, every effort should be made to hire only those best suitable for the job. This begins with the interview process, a careful background review, and a probationary period of employment to determine the employee's potential for handling the job in a satisfactory manner. Some determined action, expended at this time, will certainly be well worth the effort in terms of hiring only those individuals most suitable for the job.

One of the greatest challenges encountered with younger employees is to instill in them a sense of job ownership. The quicker they begin to understand exactly what is expected of them and to adopt a commitment to the goals and mission of the organization, the sooner they will be incorporated into the organizational structure and therefore will begin to contribute in a significant way.

Most law-enforcement organizations have some type of field training officer or program to assist newly hired employees in their first few months of the job. While a training officer is a necessary and useful function of the department, the training should not stop upon completion of the probationary period, but should continue through the implementation of a mentoring program.

One frequently encountered problem with younger employees is the tendency they often exhibit to **"reverse delegate"** tasks back to the supervisor. While it is understandable that they may be confused and even overwhelmed in taking on new assignments and projects, the supervisor should be careful not to complete the tasks for them. **It is the supervisor's job to supervise, not to do the work of employees.** When confronted with a reverse delegation attempt, the supervisor should set out the various steps of project completion, obtaining employee feedback to ensure that the steps are understood. If necessary, the supervisor should have the employee check in at various stages of the project to determine what progress is being made. Deadlines should definitely be established and monitored in this situation. The employee should have a clear understanding of what the desired result of the task will be.

Conclusion

Supervisors should be aware that their actions, decisions and even their lifestyles are being closely monitored at all times by their employees. The "Office Grapevine" is alive and well in all organizations, but it especially thrives in structured environments like public safety. Understanding this means that the supervisor is aware that associations, assignments and friendships will be scrutinized by employees for perceived favoritism. In its mildest form this will affect the efficiency of the organization, and carried to an extreme will result in employment actions or lawsuits. While in times past supervisors frequently developed "information sources" within the employment ranks, this practice is discouraged for many reasons, not the least of which includes branding the source as a "snitch" while destroying any sense of loyalty to the supervisor. Therefore, supervisors should strive to be fair at all times in their decisions and assignments, and should seek to avoid even the perception of favoritism.

Not only should supervisors treat each employee fairly, but the supervisor should go further, seeking to understand as much about the employees' personal goals, needs and family situation as possible. The more a supervisor knows about an employee's situation, personality and goals, the more effective that supervisor can be in assisting the employee to reach maximum productivity.

Building Confidence

For an organization to run efficiently, there must be a collective sense of confidence, and this sense of confidence is best built upon success. The old management cliché: "praise in public; criticize in private," is as applicable today as it was 50 years ago. While public praise is still necessary, a supervisor must be careful not to overdo public praise to the extent that it generates jealousy or foments disappointment. Generally, brief acknowledgments for a job well done are sufficient for praising in public; however, extensive praise should be extended in private.

Many supervisors and heads of organizations carry this one step further by sending personal letters (with a copy to the employee's personnel file) to the employee praising for a specific task completed, or more general praise for excellent work over a given period of time. Unlike private organizations, law-enforcement and other public organizations rarely have the financial means available to provide meaningful cash incentives. In these cases praise and recognition, along with the occasional promotion, are not only the best means of confidence building, they are the only means. Even so, supervisory recognition (and peer recognition) are often sufficient by themselves to instill and maintain a high level of organizational confidence and *esprit de corps*.

This confidence is often enhanced by involving employees in the decision-making process. This does not mean that the supervisor gives up decision-making authority, for the final decision must rest with the supervisor. In many instances, however, employees, especially those showing maturity and experience, should be invited to provide options and suggestions.

Expecting Perfection

Have you ever seen any complicated work performed to absolute perfection? It just doesn't happen in the real world and supervisors should not expect perfection even though they have a right to and should demand quality work. To demand absolute perfection in a complex task is a guarantee of failure if for no other reason than the inordinate amount of time required for completion.

Decision Making

There are a number of reasons why people, including supervisors, are reluctant to make decisions. Often they will attribute failure to make a decision upon lack of adequate information. Frequently, however, the basic reason is that they are afraid of making a mistake and they dread the consequences if a mistake is made. The Pareto Principle (80/20 rule) teaches that 80 percent of the information necessary to make a decision is obtained quickly while the remaining 20 percent is difficult to acquire. New supervisors frequently use the search for the remaining 20 percent as a rationalization for delaying a decision. A supervisor must constantly be on guard to ensure that his or her reasons for delaying decisions are not based on this search for the last 20 percent or on some other rationalization. Ultimately, supervisors must remember (or be reminded) that **they are paid to make decisions, not to avoid making them**.

Listening Skills

When asked about the most important characteristic of a leader, the head of a state Attorney General's White Collar Crime Unit stated unhesitatingly **that the ability to listen well was perhaps one of the most outstanding qualities of a leader**. Supervisors must understand that their job entails much more listening than talking. Most people communicate between 80 and 100 words per minute, but the average person can comprehend much faster than that, up to 1000 words per minute, so people often tune in and out of a conversation while retaining the ability to understand the general thread. Educators understand that the average person in a classroom setting will begin to drift mentally after 20 minutes (or less). Because of this, it takes real effort to listen intently and actively to another person. In order to do this, the listener must maintain eye contact, must exhibit signs of affirmation (head nodding, smiling), and must make a conscious effort to concentrate on what is being said. One way to maintain this concentration is to anticipate the direction in which the conversation is heading and to prepare follow up questions and comments. Another technique involves mentally summarizing the speaker's points. Active listening means just that – consciously striving to accurately understand what the speaker is attempting to communicate and often restating the points to insure the communication is understood.

Mindset of a Leader

Upon taking on a supervisory role, a leader must begin to think in terms of "we" rather than "I" or "they." One new supervisor in a small federal law enforcement office set an example that followed him for years when, upon checking into a hotel to assume his new position, he was greeted by the desk clerk who recognized his name as the incoming supervisor. The desk clerk then went on to say, "we have been expecting you. I know you work with John Jones and Jerry Thompson." The new supervisor then replied, "No, I don't work with them - they work <u>for me!</u>" The desk clerk promptly telephoned Jones and Thompson to warn them that their new supervisor had arrived and was a first class jerk. This unhappy beginning ultimately ended with the demotion and transfer of the supervisor some two years later.

Supervisors must learn quickly that they are part of a team and that any statement which could be perceived as elitist or aloof will be construed in that manner and will cause problems for the supervisor in the future.

Moving Into the Job

With training and experience, most employees begin to specialize in their chosen occupations. As they specialize, they begin to master the complexities and nuances of the job, which are so frustrating to new and inexperienced employees. Due to their skill level, they are able to handle tasks and projects which newer employees would find overwhelming. This very skill level which advanced their career as an employee may hinder it as a supervisor. People have a natural affinity for the jobs they know best, and supervisors must be on guard not to immerse themselves in the familiar details of their employee's work. They must understand that they are not assigned to do the work of the employee but to supervise the work of their employees. They have moved from the specialist or technician to the generalist and must keep a constant mental check against slipping back into the role of the specialist.

Another area of concern for the supervisor is a communication flow within the chain of command. When asked to describe and rate the various levels of communication within their office, most supervisors state that the best communication is with their peers (other supervisors), the second best communication being with their boss, and the least line of communication being with their staff (those they supervise). While this may be an accurate description of communication links in many organizations, it is certainly not the most desirable format. The optimal communication link format for any organization would be first with the staff, second with the boss, and third with peers. Closer communication with other supervisors is not desirable from an efficiency standpoint because other supervisors generally have less influence on a supervisor's career than the supervisor's staff or boss.

Finally, in communicating with others, supervisors must never forget the importance of production. From a large bureaucracy to a small law enforcement agency, every employee, no matter the position or rank, is actively producing something for a living. Therefore, every employee, from the top to the bottom of the organization, should know precisely what he or she is expected to produce. Note that this is different from knowing what he or she is to do. Production is what matters to the organization, not simply activity. So just who are the consumers of this work product and precisely how do they fit into the production scheme? Consumers are those who receive and utilize the output produced by the employee. An investigator produces a report that is received by a prosecutor. A police chief produces a budget that is received by the mayor. A corrections employee produces a report for the supervisor. Those who consume the products produced by employees are, in a real sense, customers of either the employee or the organization.

As these examples show, production, consumption and customer satisfaction are as vital in criminal justice organizations as they are in retail sales. Production, consumption and customer satisfaction, in turn, depend upon both the supervisor's ability to communicate instructions in a clear and concise manner and upon the employee's complete understanding of the instructions and successful execution of the instructions in a timely manner.

Every supervisor should constantly ask the questions, "What is my team producing?" and "Who are our consumers?" For the supervisor, communicating the answers to these questions clearly to the employees will help to establish an efficiently managed organization.

The Necessity of a Work Plan

Once instructions have been given and a basic course of action has been agreed upon, it will still be necessary to implement some method of performance evaluation. This varies widely in law enforcement and many criminal justice organizations have no existing plan for objective performance evaluation, or if a plan exists, it does so on paper only.

Without objective criteria upon which an individual's performance may be measured, promotions will be based solely upon the subjective evaluation of the rating official, which invites lawsuits for engaging in promotional actions based upon discriminatory practices.

There are many performance evaluation plans available. All of these have four common elements:

- A Standard of Performance

- Clear Lines of Authority

- A Measure of Accountability

- Employee Acceptance of the Plan

Whatever plan is chosen, there must be a clear goal that is attainable. There must be standards of measurement, such as file (performance) reviews or other methods of evaluation. When the goal is made clear to the employee, necessary tasks or action steps should be listed and definitive lines of responsibility outlined. Completion dates for major tasks must be assigned and monitored, and evaluation of the task completion undertaken.

For experienced employees, supervisors often use what is termed "Management by Exception," which allows the employee to simply notify the supervisor if the work fails to go according to the agreed-upon plan. In other words, this method recognizes the ability and efficiency of experienced employees and allows them the freedom to work without being micro-managed.

Supervisory Style: Autocrat versus Team Leader

A style of supervision often found in the criminal justice system is the autocrat, who believes in making all decisions with little or no input from employees. Employees are expressly or by implication instructed to do things in a particular way because this is the way the supervisor wants the job to be performed, not necessarily because it is an efficient way of doing things. The autocrat's way is essentially "Management by Fear."

While supervisors occasionally must play the role of the autocrat, most would be far more effective by supervising as team leaders, who generally give requests rather than commands to their employees. The team leader constantly attempts to build the unit into a cohesive team rather than mold the group into a series of individual performers. This approach assumes that the team leader's authority is understood and accepted by the employees; therefore, it is not necessary for the supervisor to gain compliance through threats, harsh words or belligerency.

There are essentially three types of decisions that every supervisor must make.

- Command decisions: those that the supervisor and only the supervisor should make.
- Consultative decisions: decisions in which the final authority rests with the supervisor, but also in which input and advice from employees is solicited.
- Group or Democratic decisions: decisions that a supervisor may safely delegate to the employees as a group.

The autocrat seldom allows group decisions or consultative decisions within the employment environment. Due to a variety of reasons, but most often because of insecurity, autocratic supervisors seldom make consultative decisions and rarely allow group decisions.

Another aspect of supervision for the 21st century is the necessity to inform employees why they are being asked to perform a certain task. It may be that the days of the autocratic leader are numbered, or it may be that they were never actually present in the United States. Our country has a long history involving the questioning of authority, so running a company or a group of employees like a medieval fiefdom may never have been the standard and may have been just as out of place 100 years ago as it is today.

Delegation

The delegation of authority and tasks is vital to the efficient management of any organizational culture. A common problem for new supervisors is essentially that of moving from a technician's job to that of an entrepreneur. Assuming the new supervisor was competent in the technician's job, it is often difficult to delegate to another person what the supervisor feels could better be done by the supervisor. As a result, the supervisor is reluctant to release control and the organization suffers from the stagnation brought on by micro management.

What can be delegated:

- Tasks that employees can do more efficiently than the supervisor.
- Tasks that employees can do at less cost than the supervisor.
- Tasks that employees can do quicker than the supervisor.
- Any task that will add to the competence of the employee.

What cannot be delegated:

- Confidential matters.
- Disciplinary matters.

The first step in delegating a task is to pick the right person for the job. The goal should be communicated to the employee in such a way that he or she will have no trouble in understanding it. It is often necessary to ask for feedback in order to ensure that the goal is understood completely. For new employees (and for some experienced employees) it is necessary to explain why the task is to be done, and occasionally even how the task is to be done. Deadlines for the completion of the task or components thereof should be set. Finally, the supervisor must follow through with evaluations, either scheduled or unscheduled.

Supervisors must constantly guard against reverse delegation, which frequently occurs with newer employees who failed to grasp the goal itself or how the goal is to be accomplished. These employees tend to seek supervisory guidance to such an extent that the supervisor ends up accomplishing the task instead of the employee.

Changing the Employee

Psychologists maintain that people change only through a traumatic experience, a religious conversion or brain surgery. That may or may not be true, but most of us understand that basic personalities rarely change. Understanding this, a supervisor may frequently alter approaches to the employee in order to find an approach that suits the employee's personality and will motivate the employee. In essence, experienced supervisors understand that what is necessary is not to change people but rather to change approaches in order to motivate people.

For detail people who are fussy about their work, supervisors generally find that it is better not to micromanage them but to harness their energy in ways which utilize their unique perspectives.

For lazy employees, the supervisor must seriously consider whether they would be more suited for some other line of work. Another question a supervisor must ask is whether or not the laziness is inherent or whether the employee is merely inefficient due to a lack of training.

When there are serious personnel problems due to alcohol or drugs, most supervisors are not capable of adequately handling the situation. Organizations today desperately need an Employee Assistance Program for situations such as these. For too long organizations have simply swept these types of problems under the rug. In order to solve problems as serious as this, the organization must confront the individual and offer help.

Finally, every organization has and must endure marginal employees. These are often longtime employees whose performance is not so bad as to warrant disciplinary action, but who are not performing at a satisfactory level, or at least at a level high enough to satisfy their supervisor. It is a fact of organizational life that the marginal employee exists in every department or unit. Much to the dismay of the supervisor, the marginal employee must be extensively supervised, trained and retrained, and even then will not produce according to expectations. This is just a basic fact that every supervisor must live with and underscores the supervisor's delight in working with those employees who are highly motivated and require little actual supervision.

Employee Discipline

Because employees are expensive to hire, train and maintain, the goal of employee discipline must be to restore the employee, not to punish. Discipline has many forms and an experienced supervisor should be careful to use only the minimal form of discipline necessary for correction and restoration.

Prior to imposing discipline, it is vital for the supervisor to seek and obtain support from above. Without the support of the supervisor's boss, the discipline will have no effect or may even be detrimental to the supervisor's career.

A lack of clear, concise rules of conduct will invite bending, stretching, and ultimately breaking of those imprecise standards that do exist. A Disciplinary Procedure Manual or Standards of Conduct is absolutely necessary to the proper functioning of any organization. This manual should be constantly reviewed for necessary additions, deletions and revisions.

Any correction deemed necessary should be imposed immediately. Failure to do so will not only undermine morale but will be counterproductive to the restorative process.

Even though discipline should be swiftly imposed, it must never be made personal. Employees should never be humiliated, because they often will return a personal attack, preventing any true corrective behavior. Criticism should be limited to the performance, not the person, and is best conducted in a conversational style while in private.

The supervisor should review both what is expected of the employee and the employee's performance. If an agreement is reached that obligates the employee to undertake certain corrective actions, a memo must be prepared by the supervisor. Those supervisors who have failed to implement this vital step have frequently regretted their inaction immensely. The axiom that "it doesn't exist if it's not in writing" certainly holds true here.

For corrective action involving attitude problems, it is often helpful to seek an admission from the employee that a problem exists. Once this has been accomplished, the employee and supervisor should jointly agree on the specifics of the problem and on steps to be taken in order to solve it. Many supervisors believe that asking the employee how the problem should be solved will initiate a dialogue and involve the employee actively in the process of its resolution. Once again, should a solution be agreed upon, a memo must be prepared in order to clarify the situation and to protect the supervisor.

Finally, supervisors should be aware that the nature of their job invites criticism from both above and below. Criticism should be looked upon as support, although few people do so. It is the rare person who can take criticism well, learn from it and prosper as a result. A corollary to criticism is failure, however, and failure should always be analyzed and treated as temporary. We all fail, and reaction to failure separates winners from losers in the end.

Sources

Banfield, Edward C. The Un-heavenly City. Boston: Little Brown and Company, 1970.

Belker, Loren B. The First Time Manager. New York: Amacom, 1997.

Bennett, Wayne W. and Karen M. Hess. Management and Supervision in Law Enforcement. Belmont, CA: Wadsworth, 2001.

Bennis, Warren, and Robert Tounsend. On Becoming a Leader. Chicago, IL: Nightingale-Conant, 1991.

Brock, T. C., Jr. "The First Line Supervisor." Federal Bureau of Investigation (undated).

Covey, Stephen R. Principle-Centered Leadership. Provo, UT: Covey Leadership Center, 1992.

Covey, Stephen R. The Seven Habits of Highly Effective People. New York: Simon and Schuster, 1989.

Fuller, George. Supervisor's Portable Answer Book. Paramus, NJ: Prentice Hall, 1990.

Hunsaker, Phillip L. and Anthony J Alessandra. The Art of Managing People. New York: Simon and Schuster, 1980.

International Association of Chiefs of Police. Managing the Small Law Enforcement Agency. Dubuque, IW: Kendall/Hunt, 1990.

Kenney, Dennis J. and Gary W. Cordner. Managing Police Personnel. Cincinnati, OH: Anderson Publishing, 1996.

Kinder, Jack, *et al*. Management Excellence. Chicago, IL: Nightingale-Conant, 1990.

Rush, Myron. Management: a Biblical Approach. Wheaton, IL: Victor Books, 1983.

Toffler, Alvin. Third Wave. New York: Bantam Books, 1981.

Waggener, H. A. and Clyde C. Schrickel, Principles of Managing. Dayton, OH: The National Management Association, 1985.

Leadership Ethics   Chapter 3

He that would govern others, first should be the master of himself. Philip Massinger, 17th Century English Dramatist

Before you read this chapter, attempt to answer this question: Why do we need a chapter on leadership ethics?

Introduction

This chapter begins by defining ethics as it applies to supervisors in criminal justice organizations. Our attention will then turn to understanding unethical behavior by examining contributing factors and remedies. As you read this chapter, attempt to apply the concepts to your particular organization and work experiences.

Definitions and Concepts of Ethics

Ethics are principles of accepted rules of conduct for a particular individual or group as mandated by law, policy, or procedure (Goodman 3). Ethics may also be defined as principles of correct or good behavior (Lynch 207). Let's take an in-depth look at these definitions.

Principles of accepted rules of conduct

- Rules are part of all facets of life.

- To a large degree rules determine how we behave.

- Rules must have consequences to be effective.

- If rules have no consequences or are not enforced, inappropriate conduct results.

For a particular individual or group

- Rules must be applied to all individuals in the same group.

- Look at a law enforcement code of ethics such as the code endorsed by the International Association of Chiefs of Police and identify the specific behaviors that are sanctioned and prohibited.

As mandated by law, policy, or procedure

- Law - U.S. Constitution, statutory laws of a state.

- Policy - SOP Manual, state personnel policies,
  Law Enforcement Code of Ethics (Bennett and Hess 301)

- Procedures - customs and traditions, rules and regulations, silent code

Exercise: List 10 specific behaviors that are unacceptable and are viewed as unethical by your employer or organization. If you are currently unemployed, pick a former employer. Also, list the origin, i.e. department policy, procedure, custom, law, of each unacceptable behavior.

<u>Unacceptable Behaviors</u>   <u>Origin</u>

Example: use of company car for personal business   Department Policy

1.

2.

3.

4.

5.

6.

8.

9.

10.

Compare your list with the behaviors identified by Dr. Tom Barker, Jacksonville State University, in his 1982 survey of police chiefs in Alabama.

Which behaviors did you list that are identified by Dr. Barker?

Which behaviors did Dr. Barker identify that were not on your list? Why?

Understanding Unethical Behavior

One approach to understanding why supervisors as well as line personnel behave inappropriately is to identify the underlying, contributing factors. These factors may be categorized as follows (Goodman 8):

E - Environment
T - Training Component
H - Home Life
I - Individual Beliefs
C - Citizens/Clients
S - Stress

Environment

An employee's environment will affect his/her attitude, beliefs, and actions.

Environment - where a person works, eats, sleeps, relaxes, worships, plays, recreates, and hangs out.

Attitude - one's disposition (major factor in a person's job satisfaction level)

Beliefs - convictions about the way things are; religious faith; trust or confidence; a creed or tenet; opinions

Actions - how one behaves; actions can be observed and measured

In-class Exercise: Select one of the following mid-level supervisors in the criminal justice system and identify his/her environment.

- A sergeant in a large metropolitan police department
- An assistant district attorney in a county of 500,000 population
- A lieutenant in a state prison
- A senior loss prevention detective in a large department store

Training Component

Criminal Justice professionals receive a variety of training before and during employment. Some criminal justice organizations such as law enforcement agencies require an applicant to pass minimum standards of performance in a structured training program. Other organizations such as private security agencies provide structured on-the-job (OJT) training to ensure employees have the necessary knowledge, skills, and abilities (KSAs) to perform their assigned tasks.

Regardless of the type of training received by an employee, the training component plays a significant role in shaping an employee's attitude toward what is acceptable behavior. Some examples of the influence of training on future employees are:

- fellow employee-trainees (peer pressure)

- instructors or mentors (supervisory models of conduct)

- command or senior staff (upper level management behavior)

Desirable ethical characteristics of instructors, mentors, or other personnel involved in the training process are professionalism, expertise, preparation, respect and courtesy.

- Professionalism
  Takes pride in self, praises effort and achievement, is firm but fair, lives the model 24 hours a day, does not use threatening or demeaning tactics, and plays the role of a mentor (role model)

- Expertise
  Possesses a high degree of knowledge, skill, and ability; attends training seminars; reads the literature; talks to other professionals about common problems; joins professional associations; continues to upgrade KSAs

- Preparation
  Arrives on the job fully prepared for work each day; is ready to handle the emotional, physical, and intellectual demands; has the "tools of the trade" readily available; avoids "winging it;" admits lack of knowledge when appropriate

- Respect and Courtesy
  Lives by the Golden Rule; shows the proper respect to all individuals with which he/she deals; does not belittle subordinates

Home Life

To fully understand the complex behaviors of subordinates, a first line supervisor must look at the past as well as the present off-duty environment (home life). The following environments are typical today:

- Living at home with parents

- Living alone

- Living with a roommate

- Living with a spouse (significant other)

- Living with a spouse and children

In-class Group Exercise: Each of these environments has significantly different influences on employees. In small group discussion, identify at least three unacceptable behaviors that may be influenced by each home life listed above. List the unacceptable behaviors that you identify during group discussion in the space after each home life environment.

The following questions pose potential conflicts between the influence of home life and job expectations. Discuss specific applications of these conflicts and suggest some ways a supervisor might provide support for an affected subordinate. List specific applications and supervisory remedies in the spaces after each question.

- What occurs when the "significant other" does not support the employee's role as a criminal justice practitioner?

- What happens when an employee finds that his/her moral training at home conflicts with job expectations? (This dilemma was described as Cognitive Dissonance by Festinger in 1957.)

- What occurs when an employee's loyalty to his/her spouse conflicts with job expectations?

Recognizing the detrimental effect of marital disharmony on job productivity, supervisors must be sensitive to their subordinates' home life. Recent studies have identified the following behaviors as major factors contributing to marital break-up: lack of time spent at home, secretive demeanor, excessive alcohol use, adultery and consumption with career.

Some possible ethical home rules are to communicate honestly with each other, discuss expectations, wear different hats, work it out and have fun.

Individual beliefs

Criminal justice employees typically enter the criminal justice work force in their early twenties. By this age they have developed specific ethical beliefs and behaviors. These beliefs and behaviors are usually a complex mix of parental training, religious influences, school experiences and a variety of other sociological factors. An effective supervisor recognizes these factors in each subordinate and is sensitive to beliefs and behaviors that may be in conflict with agency rules and regulations.

A supervisor's ethical beliefs are typically a combination of personal and professional experience. Research shows that individuals who do not support the accepted behaviors and practices of their organization typically resign or are fired in the first five years of employment. Consequently, an effective mid-level supervisor has reconciled his/her personal beliefs with his/her organization rules and regulations.

The following list of ethical beliefs exemplifies core values of our criminal justice system.

- Belief in the constitutional rights of all people.

- Belief in providing the best service of which a person is capable at all times.

- Belief in conducting oneself, on and off duty, with pride and professionalism.

- Belief in obeying all of the laws of the state and the policies of the employing agency.

- Belief in treating people fairly and without favoritism or bias.

Individual In-class Exercise: Add four more ethical beliefs to this list that you believe should be held by criminal justice professionals.

I believe _____
_____

I believe _____
_____

I believe _____
_____

I believe _____
_____

Citizens

Criminal justice practitioners constantly deal with the citizenry of their jurisdictions. For a police officer, a conflict may occur when he/she has taken an oath to protect and serve all citizens but quickly learns that all citizens are not law-abiding. A supervisor serves as a role model for his/her subordinates in dealing with the public. If a supervisor expects subordinates to avoid discrimination, bias, prejudice, and favoritism, he/she must clearly avoid these unethical behaviors.

Most employees in the criminal justice system are given a large amount of discretionary power. Each day criminal justice practitioners are faces with decisions that may be influenced by inappropriate bias and prejudice. Consider the following discretionary examples:

- Law Enforcement Officer - to make an arrest, issue a ticket, investigate an offense

- District Attorney – to prosecute, plea bargain, sentencing recommendations

- Circuit Court Judge – to accept plea bargains, set bail, set conditions of release

- Juvenile Probation Officer – to initiate a probation revocation hearing, allow travel from jurisdiction, placement in detention

In-class Group Exercise: Cite specific examples of unethical behaviors for each of the criminal justice practitioners listed above.

Stress

The ability to recognize and deal with stress in the work place presents a significant challenge to first line supervisors. While many new supervisors have learned to cope with personal stress, they are now confronted with dealing with stress factors that impact the performance of their employees. Some basic concepts regarding stress are:

- Stress refers to a physical or emotional reaction to a condition or situation.

- Stress may be viewed as good (eustress) or bad (distress), but it is still stress.

- Reactions and behaviors must be managed effectively to avoid making unethical decisions.

1. Universally recognized stressful situations are death of a loved one, divorce, serious injury or illness, separation from a marital partner, financial problems, promotion at work, anticipation of retirement, marriage, testing, and court appearances.

Conclusion

This chapter began by asking the question: "Why do we need a chapter on leadership ethics?" This question, in various forms, has been answered by numerous researchers, scholars, and practitioners, and particularly points to first line supervisors as critical personnel in determining ethical conduct of an organization. An ad hoc committee of the IACP recognized ethics as the greatest training and leadership need of law enforcement agencies in the twenty-first century. The committee's final report states,

In order to have a viable and effective integrity and ethics impact within a police organization, it is critical that an integrity and ethics emphasis be infused into an agency's policy and procedure training, supervision and accountability systems. (Ethics Training Subcommittee of the IACP Ad Hoc Committee on Police Image and Ethics 14).

The same statement could be made about any criminal justice organization today.

Sources

Bennett, Wayne W. and Karen M. Hess. Management and Supervision in Law Enforcement. Belmont, CA: Wadsworth, 2001.

Ethics Training Subcommittee of the IACP Ad Hoc Committee on Police Image and Ethics. "Ethics Training in Law Enforcement." The Police Chief, Jan. 1998: 14-24.

Glensor, Ronald W., Kenneth J. Peak and Larry K. Gaines. *Police Supervision,* Boston: McGraw-Hill, 1999.

Goodman, Debbie J. Enforcing Ethics. Upper Saddle River, NJ: Prentice Hall, 1998.

Lynch, Ronald G. The Police Manager. Cincinnati, OH: Anderson, 1998.

Case Study 3.1 – The Well-Connected Officer
(Based on Debbie J. Goodman's Enforcing Ethics)

You are a newly promoted lieutenant assigned to the patrol division of the Dog Patch Police Department. One of the officers in your division has been reprimanded for the third time for "unprofessional" conduct. Specifically, he discharged his service revolver into the hood of his patrol car while demonstrating unloading procedures to a meter maid. According to the Standard Operating Procedures of the Dog Patch PD, "Any officer who receives three reprimands is to be terminated upon notice." This officer happens to be the son of city councilman Joe Walski who has been very supportive of your department, especially during budget hearings. In fact Councilman Walski is presently serving as chair of the committee considering pay raises for Dog Patch PD.

Dog Patch Police of Chief Oscar Meyer calls you into his office and asks for your recommendation in this personnel matter.

1. What recommendation/s do you make to the Chief Meyer?

2. Why did you make this recommendation/s?

3. What is the overriding ethical principle/s that guided your decision?

4. After you leave the Chief's office, you encounter Councilman Walski outside the police department. Councilman Walski recognizes you as his son's superior officer and asks you for information about the matter. How do you respond? Be specific.

Case Study 3.2 – Traffic Assist
(Based on Debbie J. Goodman's Enforcing Ethics)

You are a shift sergeant at the Walla Walla Police Department. Officer Green, a recent training academy graduate, enters your office, closes the door and tells you that he has a "hypothetical" problem. He informs you, just hypothetically, that another officer may have received $20 from a motorist for changing his tire. The officer came upon an elderly gentleman during a rainstorm who was feebly attempting to change a flat tire. This "hypothetical" officer quickly changed the tire while the elderly man sat in his car staying dry and warm. Before the officer left, the elderly man reached into his pocket and pulled out a $20. When the officer refused the money, the man said that he would have spent $50 to get wrecker service and sat in the bad weather several hours. The man insisted that the officer take the money as a token of his appreciation for the kindness shown to him by the officer. The man said that he would be very offended if the officer did not accept his complimentary gesture.

Officer Green's question is "How should this officer handle situations like this?"

Goal Setting — Chapter 4

The tragedy of life doesn't lie in not reaching your goal. The tragedy lies in having no goals to reach.   Benjamin Mays

What you get by achieving your goals is not as important as what you become by achieving your goals.   Zig Ziglar

---

In Lewis Carrol's *Alice in Wonderland*, Alice encounters the Cheshire Cat at a fork in the road. She asks the Cat, "would you tell me, please, which way I ought to go from here?" The Cat answers, "that depends a good deal on where you want to get to." "I don't much care where," said Alice, to which the Cat replied, "Then it doesn't matter which way you go."

This story illustrates the situation of most Americans who encounter daily crossroads along the path of life. Because they have no clear idea about their goals in life, they wander along aimlessly, choosing any fork that looks appealing at the time, without thinking about their destination and whether taking the chosen road will lead them there. As a result, few can look back on a finished career with a satisfaction that they have done their best, or even close to their best, in their chosen field.

Students who diligently apply the principles learned in this course can expect to have clear, concise, written goals and should expect to gain at least one hour per day to gain the goals they have set.

The first recommendation is to arise at least one hour earlier each workday to prepare for the future. This sounds so simplistic but could have a dramatic impact on the life of any person who does this.

If individuals spent just one hour per day reading in their chosen field, they would find the following benefits:

- Over 300 hours per year would be spent reading in their field.

- This would equal over 37 workdays per year - over an extra month of working.

- They could easily read 25 books in a year.

- In 5 years, they would have read over 100 books.

- They would be a recognized expert in the field.

- This should make them much more productive, which translates into faster promotions.

See the following chart to determine the value of your time:

If You Earn:	Every Minute is Worth:	Every Hour Is Worth:	In a Year, One Hour a Day is Worth:
$2,000	$0.0170	$1.02	$250
2,500	$0.0213	1.28	312
3,000	$0.0256	1.54	375
3,500	$0.0300	1.79	437
4,000	$0.0341	2.05	500
5,000	$0.0426	2.56	625
6,000	$0.0513	3.07	750
7,000	$0.0598	3.59	875
7,500	$0.0640	3.84	937
8,000	$0.0683	4.10	1,000
8,500	$0.0726	4.35	1,063
10,000	$0.0852	5.12	1,250
12,000	$0.1025	6.15	1,500
14,000	$0.1195	7.17	1,750
16,000	$0.1366	8.20	2,000
20,000	$0.1708	10.25	2,500
25,000	$0.2135	12.81	3,125
30,000	$0.2561	15.37	3,750
35,000	$0.2988	17.93	4,375
40,000	$0.3415	20.49	5,000
50,000	$0.4269	25.61	6,250
75,000	$0.6403	38.42	9,375
100,000	$0.8523	51.23	12,500

Based on 244 eight-hour working days.

from *Working Smart*, Michael Leboeuf, PHD

Why should you care about Goal Setting?

Examine the Time Management Matrix:

Time Management Matrix

	Urgent	Not Urgent
Important	**I** ACTIVITIES: Crises Pressing Problems Deadline-Driven Projects	**II** ACTIVITIES: Prevention, PC Activities Relationship Building Recognizing New Opportunities Planning Recreation
Not Important	**III** ACTIVITIES: Interruptions, Some Calls Some Mail, Some Reports Some Meetings Close, Not Pressing Matters Popular Activities	**IV** ACTIVITIES: Trivia, Busy Work Some Mail Some Phone Calls Time Wasters Pleasant Matters

Source: <u>The Seven Habits of Highly Effective People</u>, by Stephen R. Covey

Where do most employees spend their time?

Where should most employees spend their time?

In order to achieve goals, individuals must have clear, written goals. Less than three percent of Americans have written goals, and these are generally considered the most successful people in their fields. The starting point is to understand precisely what you want to accomplish and then to arrange your life around the steps necessary to achieve that accomplishment.

As time management expert Brian Tracy states, "Time management more than anything else means the planning and organizing of your time in such a way that you accomplish your most important goals as quickly as possible."

Basic Principles of Goal Setting:

Goals must be balanced:

- Personal Goals

- Professional Goals

- Preparation Goals (Steps necessary to achieve the personal and professional goals)

- Purpose Goal: The one goal that if achieved gives your life purpose and meaning.

Goal Setting Exercise:

1. List all the goals you would like to achieve over the next five years (It makes no difference which goal you choose -- list them all).

2. Classify Goals as A, B or C, with A goals being basically life changing, B goals being very important but not life changing, and C goals being somewhat important but not as important as either A or B goals.

3. Examine all the A goals and rank them as A-1, A-2, etc., with A-1 being the most important life changing goal.

4. Examine the stated A-1 goal and list all the steps necessary to achieve this goal.

5. Examine these steps and place them in the sequential order in which they must be accomplished for the goal to be met.

6. Complete steps four and five for each one of the A goals you have listed.

7. Undertaking this exercise provides clear, written goals, organized in terms of priority. Those who succeed in setting written goals, will then be in the top three percent of Americans having an understanding of where they are going and how they are going to get there.

Just having goals is not enough, however. For an individual to reach the goals, there must be constant reminders (in written form) to achieve the steps outlined. In other words, something must be done every day toward the achievement of the set goals. This would include mentally picturing the goal and acting as if the goal achievement were inevitable.

Management by Objectives

As we have stated, Management by Objectives (MBO) is a commonly used tool by supervisors to determine job performance of employees. It can also be used to measure one's own performance in achieving goals.

Steps in the MBO process include :

1. Clearly defining the desired goal.

2. Agreeing on the method of implementation; in other words, reaching an agreement on the steps necessary to successfully complete the task.

3. Agreeing specifically on a time frame for the completion – setting deadlines.

4. Providing enough support for the employee to complete the task, which includes leaving the employee alone so that the goal may be reached.

5. As a corollary to this rule, experienced employees should receive minimum supervision if they have displayed competence in similar tasks. This is sometimes referred to as "Management by Exception."

Goal Attainment Considerations

Has the goal been reduced to writing? If so, there are other considerations which must be addressed, such as:

1. Obstacles preventing the goal attainment.

2. Identifying the Limiting Step. This is the factor that sets the speed at which the goal can be reached. There is always at least one Limiting Step, and there may be more than one.

3. Knowledge items -- that which must be known or learned to reach the goal.

4. Identities of those individuals who have the ability to help reach the goal as well as those who have the ability to prevent the goal from being reached.

With every important goal, especially those that are complex, each of the above considerations should be regarded and, if appropriate, solutions found to overcome the considerations.

Sources

Bennis, Warren, and Robert Tounsend. On Becoming a Leader. Chicago, IL: Nightingale-Conant, 1991.

Covey, Stephen R. Principle-Centered Leadership. Provo, UT: Covey Leadership Center, 1992.

Covey, Stephen R. The Seven Habits of Highly Effective People. New York: Simon and Schuster, 1989.

Covey, Stephen R. First Things First. New York: Simon and Schuster, 1994.

LeBoeuf, Michael. Working Smart. New York: Warner Books, 1979.

Tracy, Brian. How to Master Your Time. Chicago, IL: Nightingale-Conant, 1989.

Time Management   Chapter 5

Until we can manage TIME, we can manage nothing else. Peter F. Drucker

Teach us to number our days aright, that we may gain a heart of wisdom. Psalm 90:12

In Chapter Four, we learned about the importance of goal setting to your personal and professional life. Understanding that goals are needed and even setting goals will not guarantee the goals will be achieved. We now understand that goal setting and goal achieving take time and energy, and individuals must actively devote time and energy for their achievement.

The question then becomes one of how this will be done. There is no magic formula; however, there are techniques available which teach how to manage time in such a way to be more productive within a given period. Increasing productivity (at least in theory) will free available time to devote to skill development, learned skill application, and finally, to goal achievement.

Organization

Time management begins with organization. There is no way that most individuals could structure their lives to gain one extra hour per day for personal and professional development without first restructuring their daily life. In order to discover how much restructuring you need in your professional life, answer the questions concerning the File Audit below (students who have not yet entered the workplace may substitute personal or course work):

*FILE AUDIT**

1. Can you retrieve any paper from your desk-side files within three minutes?

2. Can your secretary or clerical assistants retrieve papers from the office files within five minutes of your request?

3. Are backup materials for a report generally stored compactly in a few folders, or scattered randomly in many folders?

4. Have you ever "winged" a report because backup materials were lost in the files?

5. Do you often keep papers longer than two years "just in case" you might need them someday?

6. Do any file headings, other than proper or "tag" names, start with a date or adjective (e.g., "1979 Reports" or "Old Plans")?

7. Other than cross-reference copies, are duplicates of one document likely to be found in several different files?

8. Would it take more than half an hour to file the papers in your "to file" box or folder?

9. Are broad categories (travel, for instance) broken down into many minor subdivisions (travel agents, hotels, restaurants, client addresses, car services, etc,)?

Scoring: Questions 1-3:   7 points for each "no."
          Questions 4-9:   5 points for each "yes."

IF YOUR SCORE IS

0-10   Your system is efficient, although it may benefit from additional fine-tuning.

11-25 Missing papers have probably caused anxiety more than once. File review and reorganization may be advisable.

26-51 Your system is an absolute disaster! Reorganization is not a luxury, but a necessity.

*Winston, Stephanie. <u>The Organized Executive</u>. New York: Warner Books, 1983

First steps to becoming organized:

- Clean up and organize your workspace. Studies have shown that executives prefer to promote people with clean desks over people with messy desks.

- Clear your desk of everything but the task you are working on

- Assemble all the tools and information you need before beginning your work.

- Resolve to handle each paper or document only once: former Mayor Emory Folmar, Montgomery, Alabama, believes that this is the single most important principle in Time Management.

Incoming Mail

Next, a system should be devised to handle incoming mail. One of the best systems (and perhaps the simplest) may be found in *The Organized Executive*, by Stephanie Winston. She calls it the TRAF System. With this system, each incoming paper, letter or file is scanned for content and then placed in one of four areas using the following guidelines:

- **Toss** – (in trash can) Ask yourself, "If I didn't read this would there be any negative results?" If not, you can most likely toss the item.

- **Refer** - (Delegate) Is there someone who could better handle this?

- **Action** Folder - for items you must handle now.

- **File** - (in a permanent file), but ask, "What happens if I tossed this?" If the consequences are little, then toss, but if needed in the future, then file.

Assume that you work for a medium-sized law enforcement agency. Utilizing the **TRAFF** system, determine the appropriate way to handle each one of the following items and be prepared to defend your reasons for the choice:

- For Your Information (FYI) Weekly Crime Reports: _____

- Budget data for your squad or section: _____

- Flyer about a training class you will not attend: _____

- Changes to the Department Policy Manuel: _____

- New criminal on consent searches: _____

- Your Boss sends you an old copy of an employee's evaluation and says to update by next month: _____

When you finish working, put the papers away. Always began and end with a clean workspace. Make a habit of putting things away.

Time Management Tools

1. Time Planners, such as Day Timer or Day Runner. These should contain:

- A Master list for each goal, task and required action as they arise.

- A Calendar that enables the user to set dates several months (and even a year or so) in advance.

- A Daily To Do List. – This is a "must have" item. Write in this list every single thing you expect to do over the course of the day. Studies show that workplace efficiency can be increased over 25% by just using the To Do List. New things must be written on list as they come up.

    o The activities on the list should be prioritized.

    o Time planners must recognize the difference between the urgent and the important. The urgent is seldom important and the important is seldom urgent.

    o Give priority to those tasks that are both urgent and important.

    o Use following system to prioritize:
      - A - Very important, must do.
      - B - Important, should do.
      - C - Not Important but nice to do.
      - D - Delegate (Refer).
      - E - Eliminate.

Once the items have been ranked in order of importance, locate the item on the list which is more important than all the others put together. Begin here.

Your To Do List is a blueprint for the day. Do nothing until you have entered and ranked the proposed item.

2. A Tickler System.

- A tickler system does just what its name implies. It is a reminder (or tickler) of important events, files or tasks.

- One such system is called The 45 file System. In this system the originator sets up 31 files (usually hanging files or accordion files) numbered 1-31 for the days of the month. Behind these are twelve monthly files, and last are two yearly files.

    - Items or tasks are placed in the corresponding numbered day file; for example, a work project that is due on the 17th of this month is placed in file 17. Projects that are due to be begun within the next year are placed in the matching monthly file and, when that month arrives, they are transferred from the monthly file to the matching day file. Projects that are scheduled to begin next year or the year after are placed in the corresponding yearly files.

    - This system works well for those supervisors who have no computer access (or no computer skills). It also lends itself to many short term tasks. When the files and other items are transferred from the monthly area to the matching dates of the current month, they should be reviewed carefully to determine priority and the time necessary for completion.

- Daily Planning should begin the night before by preparing the next day's list. This should normally be the last thing done before leaving the work area at night.

3. Permanent Files

These are useful at home or in the office and work with either manila or hanging file systems. Most file systems work best if they are in alphabetical order, filed according to the most important name. For extensive files, a master list should be kept giving the title and location of every file. A Rolodex or computer database, if kept up to date, will make an excellent master list. If no master list is used, cross referencing can be helpful by placing copies of the item under several file headings. For example, a letter from Officer John Jones of the Crosstown Police Department should be filed under both Jones and Crosstown.

For often used items, separate, broad category files should be made, such as personal items, office policy, firearms, and legal items.

Be sure to include a Temporary Items File. Place items that have an obvious expiration date in this file. Temporary files should be purged on a periodic basis.

Other Ideas to Consider

- Do Creative work during your internal prime time. If possible, plan your day so your most important projects will be handled during your personal best working time. Most of us work best at a particular period of the day. That is why we use the term, "morning person" or "night person."

- Dictate your correspondence rather than typing or hand writing it. Of course, in many organizations, secretarial staff is scarce and many employees, including supervisors, are expected to type their own work. Serious consideration should be given to using voice recognition software in this case. The software, while not perfect, can certainly increase the speed at which work is produced, and can often cut typing time by half or better. In all but the deluxe editions the software is affordable for the average person, often costing less than $50, and even the least expensive versions include headset microphones.

- For those who often travel by air, productive work can usually be achieved by sitting in a window seat where an emergency exit is located. Emergency exit seats usually have a few inches of extra legroom and sitting next to a window insures fewer disruptions.

- Think about the future impact of the action you are preparing to undertake. If it is important it will have a future impact. Low priority items have no consequences - this will give you an idea of what is important and what you should be doing.

- Consider your own talents; what accounts for your successes; where can you outperform your peers?

- In what parts of your job do you perform better than others? How can you concentrate on these areas?

- In What areas does your organization excel?

- Does the 80/20 rule apply to your organization? Do you focus your time on the first 20 percent of the task? The first 20 percent of time on a task usually accounts for 80 percent of the value of the task.

- Who are the most important clients (consumers) or potential clients?

- Consider setting up Organizational Triage. Triage was a system developed during World War I to divide wounded soldiers into those that were dying, those who would heal without treatment, and those who might have a chance to live if given priority medical treatment. The thinking at the time was that this system automatically saved more lives than if all wounded soldiers received equal medical treatment. The same principle may also be applied in the criminal justice field. For example, one local office of the FBI set up a form of Organizational Triage, dividing cases into those which would probably be solved with little work, those which probably would not be solved despite extraordinary efforts to do so, and those which, although complex, might be solved if extra resources were devoted to them. By concentrating on the first and third group, the Bureau developed a more efficient way of utilizing limited investigative resources to handle an ever increasing number of cases.

Habits of Highly Productive People

- Most people only work at 40 percent of their maximum effectiveness.

- Focus and Concentration. There is a difference between the two in that focus has been described as clarity about the needed results, while concentration is the ability to stay with the task until completion. In order to make effective use of time an individual must have the ability to both focus and concentrate on a particular project.

- Four Steps to High Productivity

    o Set Clear Goals in Writing. Ask yourself what you are trying to do with this particular project and how you are trying to do it.

    o Create a Detailed Plan of Action that answers the above questions.

    o Set Clear Priorities with activities organized in a hierarchy of value and importance to the needed result with the 80/20 rule in mind.

    o Began with Single Minded Concentration on the highest priority task to get to the goal.

- Six keys to develop concentration:

    o Clear your workspace of everything except what is necessary to complete the job.

    o Plan your days through blocks of time with a minimum of 60-90 minutes each. Often working in the early morning is best. Before work, during lunch and after work is also good.

    o The last 20 percent of the time block often contains 80 percent of the most productive time.

    o Steady, concentrated effort is necessary for productive work.

    o Create a reward system for yourself on completion of each task, especially those that you consider difficult.

    o Resolve to finish the task on which you are currently working.

- Seven Ideas to increase productivity:

    o Concentrate on a few major areas where efforts will bring maximum results.

    o Do the things that you are better at doing.

    o Identify and concentrate on your key result areas.

- o Use deadlines on your important goals and stick to them.

- o Promise others you will finish by the deadline. This is a great motivator because if you announce to the world that you will accomplish something, you will be more likely to put forth maximum effort to finish by the deadline date.

- o Take the time to do the job well. Maintain an even pace and work steadily.

- More ways to save time:

    - o Plan your work calls geographically.

    - o Do all of your errands at one time.

    - o Be punctual - if you are not early, you are late.

Time Wasters

- Telephone interruptions. Use telephones as business tools only. They should not be used for socializing (at least excessively). The only exception to this would be when the socializing is actually networking (more on this later).

    - o If possible, have your calls screened or held.

    - o Use call-back times -- determined when you can return calls or advise the calling party when you will be available to take a call.

    - o Plan your calls in advance and make an outline of the items to be discussed.

    - o Take careful notes when making important calls. Many law-enforcement agencies want notes dictated within a few working days. This insures the information covered in the notes will still be fresh in the mind of the person dictating. This is an excellent rule to follow, as anyone who has tried to rebuild information from old notes is aware.

- Drop in visitors.

    - It is best to specify a quiet time for many tasks in which visitors are not accepted. People often use areas other than their office for tasks such as dictating. It is not unusual in criminal justice to find people working on projects in other offices, in their cars and at courthouses.

    - When drop in visitors are encountered, experts often advise that they be greeted by standing up when they enter in the office, and the greeter should remain standing during the conversation so as not to invite the visitor for a long stay.

    - Arrange appointment times.

    - Of course, you should also try to avoid dropping in on others without an appointment.

Crisis Management

Preparing for crises involves asking what can go wrong and how we will handle the situation when it occurs. This should be done frequently with every important job related subject (and is not a bad idea to incorporate in our personal lives either). Crisis management involves planning for anticipated crises and should a crisis occur, the following steps should be included in handling it:

- Have a written plan. This would include analyzing anticipated crises and listing steps to solve them. These plans should be updated frequently.

- Stop and think before acting. Often our first reactions are instinctive and are not the best solution.

- Delegate action whenever possible. It is difficult to micromanage a serious crisis – you will need help, so never be afraid to ask for it.

- Ask questions and get enough facts to understand the crisis before acting.

- Deal with recurring crises through delegation so others can handle them in your absence. This implies updates or changes to your departmental policy manual or procedures.

Procrastination

- Types of Procrastination:

    - Internal. This involves Attitude Procrastination, where an individual just can't get motivated, or Cognitive Block, where an individual simply does not have the knowledge or skills necessary to complete the work.

    - External. External procrastination includes environmental factors such as cluttered desks or work areas, lack of proper tools, physical problems, fatigue, stress or illness.

- Root Causes of Most Procrastination:

    - Fear, often a fear of failure.
        - This seems strange because we usually learn more from failure than from success.

        - The way to deal with Fear:
            - Discover what the fear is; analyzing fear can often lead to successful methods of dealing with it.

            - This involves being honest about the situation.

            - And may involve conquering fear by acting like you have overcome it, similar to the old Barbizon modeling advertisements: "You too can be a model, or just act like one."

    - Socializing.
        - Should be overcome socializing only at coffee breaks, lunch or after work.

- Relationships with knowledge workers are an exception to this rule, but the time must be watched so that focus can be maintained.

- Tips for Overcoming Procrastination:

    o Set deadlines for all important tasks, and advise others of the deadlines.

    o Don't make excuses for failure to complete tasks on time.

    o Create a reward system for each phase of the work and the job as a whole. Even small rewards work here.

    o Accept all responsibility for the completion of a given task.

    o Before undertaking any work:
        - Prioritize each part of the plan in written steps.
        - Clear the workspace area of unnecessary items.
        - Gather all necessary tools needed for the job.
        - Start with tasks that are both urgent and important.
        - Deliberately procrastinate on non-important tasks in favor of important tasks.

    o Techniques for getting started:
        - Salami slice the task (do one small part to start).
        - Use the Swiss Cheese technique by selecting a small part of the job (in the beginning, middle or end) and do it. This is called punching a hole in the job.
        - Do the task that causes you the most anxiety. Start the day with the most unpleasant task first.
        - Think of the negative consequences of not doing the job, and all the reasons for completing the job.
        - Set aside a designated period of the day when you will work on your project and nothing else.

- Don't worry about doing the job perfectly, just get started!

Keeping up with your field

The amount of knowledge in each field is doubling every seven years. At least this is the conventional wisdom. In the technology area, most knowledge is vastly outdated by that time (think computers and software).

Moore's Law, formulated in 1965 by the man who later co-founded Intel (now the world's largest manufacturer of microprocessor chips), currently suggests that the number of transistors that can be fitted on to a chip doubles roughly every 18 months. This has remained amazingly true since its discovery. Translated in real world terms, this means that as the ability of technology to store, compute and transmit data has expanded, so has the useful application of that data concurrently expanded in ways that significantly change our lives. Technology, without practical application, is useless however, so practical application of ever-changing technology is the key to advancement in today's working environment.

So how do we keep current in our field?

- Read one hour per day in your chosen field, and take notes.

- Read business and trade publications in your field.

- Invest 3% of your income on training.

- Read business magazines, such as Success, Inc., and Forbes.

- Some experts advise that for magazines and journals, the reader should read the table of contents, find articles of interest and tear them out, carrying them to read during transition time. This avoids the time wasted by reading the publication cover to cover.

- Read books by experts in their fields - practical experts, not theorists. Textbooks often impart knowledge by theorists, not practical application, so look for books written by people who are experienced in their fields.

- Read paperbacks because they have already been chosen as the best of the hardbacks.

- Underline key passages and have them transcribed or use voice recognition software to transcribe them yourself.

- Join book clubs in your field: Executive Book Club, Fortune Book Club and Quality Book Club. They feature the best of the management and leadership books each year.

- Join Book Condensation Services, such as Soundview Executive Book Summaries, McMillan Executive Book Summaries, or Fasttrack Executive Audio Summaries.

- Learn How to read a book efficiently. Most people are surprised to learn that (for business or technical books) reading cover to cover is not the best way to read and learn the contents. A better method is the OPIR System:

    o Overview: look at front and back cover and the table of contents: flip through quickly to get overview,

    o Preview: flip through again, stopping and reading an occasional sentence or part of paragraphs,

    o In-view: using hands to quickly turn pages, go through page by page scanning to fill in gaps,

    o Review: read the important parts.

- Listen to audio cassettes in your car. The average person spends three to six months in a car, the same as one to two university semesters.

- Attend all the training seminars and courses you are given the opportunity to attend. These usually consist of distilled information that can be quickly digested and put into practice.

- Join professional associations and self-help groups. Most successful persons in their professions are the ones involved in helping others.

- Network with others in the field. This is so important that a separate section on Networking will be included in this book.

- Get up one hour early and invest the time in yourself.

- Plan every day in advance - in writing.

Sources

Covey, Stephen R. <u>The Seven Habits of Highly Effective People</u>. New York: Simon and Schuster, 1989.

Covey, Stephen R. <u>First Things First</u>. New York: Simon and Schuster, 1994.

Tracy, Brian. <u>How to Master Your Time</u>. Chicago, IL: Nightingale-Conant, 1989.

Winston, Stephanie. <u>The Organized Executive</u>. New York: Warner Books, 1983.

Motivation   Chapter 6

Individual commitment to a group effort – that is what makes a team work, a company work, a society work, a civilization work.   Vince Lombardi, Green Bay Packers Football Coach

Introduction

In this chapter we will define motivation, introduce some related concepts, and then apply six theories of motivation to situations commonly faced by the criminal justice first line supervisor.

Motivation is one of the more important aspects of human behavior in criminal justice organizations. The study of motivation attempts to answer the question, "Why do individuals behave in a particular way?" The study of motivation theories provides criminal justice students with a framework of ideas from which to test their understanding of behavior and, more specifically, to understand what motivates people to work.

Definitions

Motivation has something to do with 1) the direction of behavior, 2) the strength of the effort put forth once an individual chooses a course of action, and 3) the persistence of the behavior.

> Motivation is an inner state that causes an individual to behave in a way that ensures the accomplishment of some goal (Glensor, Peak and Gaines 41).

> Motivation cannot be measured but can be inferred from behavior.

> Motivation is an important factor in individual performance.

Related Concepts

Performance is influenced by an individual's ability.

Performance = ability x motivation

Ability can be defined as an individual's talent for accomplishing work-related tasks.

Employees will not perform to their ability levels unless they are sufficiently motivated.

Good managers must know how to motivate individuals to perform well.

Therefore, a basic knowledge of motivation theories is necessary.

Theories of Motivation

Motivational theories may be grouped into two general categories: content theories and process theories.

Content theories attempt to identify what in the work environment motivates behavior (money, social interaction, growth needs). They are Needs Hierarchy Theory, Two-Factor Theory, and Achievement Motivation Theory.

Process theories describe how motivation is translated into behavior. They are Expectancy Theory, Equity theory, and Goal-Setting Theory.

Discussion Question: Why is it necessary for first line supervisors to understand basic theories of motivation?

Maslow's Hierarchy of Needs

The first content theory of motivation is Abraham H. Maslow's Hierarchy of Needs (1943). The following table shows the five levels of needs and their application to the criminal justice work place. As you review the table below, think of examples from your employment history and attempt to apply your examples to this model of motivation. For example, do you recall jobs that only met physiological and safety needs?

Hierarchy of Needs	Related Work Needs
Self-Actualization	Challenging work opportunities for innovation and problem solving, training, and development
Esteem Needs	Important work, recognition, promotion
Social Needs	Good relations with colleagues, supervisors, and the public
Safety Needs	Job security, benefits including health and life insurance
Physiological Needs	Basic pay, equipment, workspace

Maslow argues that each level of needs must be satisfied at least in part before a person can move to the next level of needs. Applying that concept to the related work needs identified above, a worker will not attempt to establish good relationships at the workplace until his/her safety and physiological needs are met. What do you think about this theory?

Group Discussion Question:

Can you recall a specific time when a fellow employee or subordinate was requesting additional training and more challenging assignments at the same time he/she was receiving base pay with poor or inadequate equipment and workspace?

Maslow argues that a person cannot reach the self-actualization needs level without satisfying all of the lower levels. Do you agree or disagree? Why?

Herzberg's Two-Factor Theory

The second content theory of motivation is Frederick Herzberg's Two-Factor Theory (1959) (Gibson, Ivancevich, and Donnelly 118). These two factors are hygiene factors (conditions that are external to the job such as pay) and motivating factors (conditions that are built into the job itself such as advancement). The following table provides further descriptions of these factors. As you read these factors, try to remember what motivated you to become a criminal justice practitioner or obtain a specific job.

Hygiene Factors	*Motivating Factors*
Factors That Help to Prevent job Dissatisfaction	Factors That Help to Promote Satisfaction
Company Procedures	Achievement
Quality of supervision	Recognition
Salary	The Work Itself
Status	Responsibility
Working Conditions	Advancement
Job security	Growth

Group Discussion Questions:
1. Which of the factors listed above motivated you to apply for your current job?

2. What do you think motivates individuals to apply for criminal justice jobs today? Have these motives changed during the past 20 years?

3. Why do some employees fail to seek promotion and/or refuse to become supervisors?

4. What perceptions of your current job did you have prior to employment that you later found to be unrealistic?

The Herzberg model helps us to categorize motivations and determine if pre-employment job expectations are being met by employers. This approach to understanding motivation requires a supervisor to look retrospectively at motivations. Can employees be aware of all conditions that motivated or dissatisfied them (House and Wigdon 441)?

McClelland's Achievement Motivation Theory

The third and final content theory of motivation is David McClelland's Achievement Motivation Theory (1962). This motivation theory provides a supervisor with criteria to identify the performance of high achievers and what action supervisors need to take to encourage continued high performance.

This theory also recognizes that some employees are highly motivated to accomplish more that their fellow workers. Some employees seem to be satisfied just by doing the minimum work in order to retain their job and not be criticized by supervisors. The high achiever employee presents a unique challenge to management. If this worker is properly managed, the organization meets his/her needs and increases overall productivity.

Profile of High Achievers	Action of Management
Prefer to set their own performance goals	Encourage subordinates to think realistically
Prefer to avoid easy and difficult performance goals	Give subordinates moderate challenges and responsibilities
Prefer immediate and reliable feedback	Arrange tasks so subordinates receive periodic feedback
Like to be responsible for solving problems	Publicize accomplishments

Discussion Questions:

Have you ever supervised or worked with an employee who fits the above profile? If so, how did you or your supervisor handle the high achiever?

How are high achievers in your current job perceived by members of your organization?

What is the education level of the high achievers in relation to the other members of your work group?

How would you rate the work satisfaction level of the high achievers as compared to other members of your work group?

Vroom's Expectancy Theory

The first <u>process</u> theory of motivation is Victor Vroom's Expectancy (1964). Vroom defines motivation as a process governing choices among alternative forms of voluntary activity. A person has an expectancy (or belief) that a chance exists that a certain effort will lead to a particular level of performance. The person further believes that this performance leads to certain outcomes. These relationships may be viewed as follows:

Effort >>>> Performance >>> Outcome

Basic Expectancy Theory Concepts:

Employees have expectations about what outcomes are likely to result from their behavior.
Application: Most employees are made aware of job expectations during training and/or orientation. For instance an employee is advised that he must be at his workstation at promptly
8 a.m. Monday through Friday. This employee understands this job requirement means that he must get up, prepare for work and travel to his job site (effort) by 8 a.m. (performance) if he wishes to keep his job (outcome).

Expectancy refers to the employees' belief that a particular behavior will be followed by a particular outcome.

Application: "If I work hard (particular behavior), I will receive a pay increase or a promotion (particular outcome)."

Employees have different preferences among these outcomes.
Application: Some employees want more pay (outcome) while others want more time off the job (outcome).

The strength of a person's belief that certain performance will lead to certain outcomes determines how much effort the person puts into his/her performance.
Application: If an employee strongly believes (due to past experiences, promises from his supervisor, written agency communications) that he will receive a raise if he puts in 10 hours of unpaid overtime each week, he may make the effort to receive the raise.

Vroom also argues that the strength of an individual's desire for a particular outcome will determine how much effort is exerted.
Application: If a person has a strong need to get off work next Friday, he/she will do whatever it takes to achieve this goal.

Adam's Equity Theory

The second process theory is J. Stacey Adams' Equity Theory of motivation (1963). His theory is based on the fundamental principle of equality in the workplace. In the public sector equity means that workers are treated fairly without bias or prejudice. This concept is supported by rules, regulations and laws at all levels of government. In the private sector individuals measure their performance with fellow workers and expect similar compensation for their efforts. The table below shows the process that motivates employees to accomplish tasks at a specific level of achievement.

Employee has inputs and receives outcomes	Employee is aware of other employee inputs and outcomes	Employee compares his inputs and outcomes	Employee perceives equity or inequity
Inputs: Skills, experience, training, race, gender	Outcomes: Pay, benefits, recognition, promotion	Stimulus	Equity: Ratio is equivalent Inequity: imbalance exists

The above model opines that employees are aware of the knowledge, skills and ability (KSAs) they bring to the workplace. They are also aware of the KSAs and performance levels of fellow employees to some extent. Adam's argues that employees frequently compare their performance levels with that of fellow workers and may be motivated to not work as hard if they perceive an inequity.

Equity theory has two major premises regarding individual motivation:

    1 - the perception of inequity creates tension, and

    2 - this tension makes people want to reduce or eliminate the inequity.

An individual might be motivated to put in less unpaid overtime or not produce as much in order to reduce the tension created by the perception of inequity. In other words, an individual who perceives that he is not being treated in the same manner as his follow workers, is likely to makes adjustment in his level of performance.

Locke's Goal-Setting Theory

The third content theory of motivation is E.A. Locke's Goal-Setting Theory. The table below lists some goal setting concepts and their inherent problems.

Theory	Problems
Goals are primary determinants of behavior	Goal setting is complex
Harder goals result in higher performance	Goal setting can encourage game playing
Goal setting directs attention	Goal accomplishment can become an obsession
Goal setting increases persistence	Goal setting can be used as a control devise
Goal setting works well for simple jobs	Goal setting works less well for complex jobs

Discussion Questions:
Do you set personal performance goals? Name them.

Does your immediate supervisor set goals for you? Name them.

Does your supervisor set unrealistic goals for you or your work group to meet? Why are they unrealistic?

Summary

In this chapter we have presented several definitions of motivation and some related concepts. More than any other personnel manager, the first line supervisor must understand the dynamics of human behavior motivation. An understanding of content and process theories provide a supervisor with an array of causal explanations for the lack of performance in some employees and the excessive performance of others. Human behavior is complex and no one theory of motivation has been found to explain motivation of employees. Each of the theories presented in this chapter brings some insight into the challenges faced by the first line supervisor in motivating his/her subordinates.

Sources

Cordner, Gary W. and Robert Sheehan. Police Administration. Cincinnati, OH: Anderson, 1999.

Gibson, James l., John M. Ivancevich and James H. Donnelly, Jr. Organizations. Homewood, Illinois: BPI Irwin, 1988.

Lynch, Ronald G. The Police Manager. Cincinnati, OH: Anderson, 1998.

Peak, Kenneth J. Justice Administration. Englewood Cliffs, NJ: Prentice Hall, 1995.

Communication   Chapter 7

Some persons talk simply because they think sound is more manageable than silence.
Margaret Halsey

While the right to talk may be the beginning of freedom, the necessity of listening is what makes the right important. Walter Lippmann, U.S. Newspaper Commentator

Introduction

Communication is one of the most important dynamics of an organization. Quite often problems in organizations can be traced to the lack of effective communication. With this much importance it is difficult to understand why organizations fail to provide proper communication training to its employees, particularly the first line supervisor. Bennett and Hess suggest that supervisors spend 15% of their time with superiors and 50% with subordinates (76). A large portion of each supervisor's day whether she is a corrections lieutenant, police sergeant or squad supervisor for the FBI is spent in some form of communication.

This chapter presents some basic concepts for first line supervisors. We begin with basic communication concepts, applying them to usage by supervisors, and then consider some models and theories of communication that impact the first line supervisor.

Basic Concepts

- Fish gotta swim. Birds gotta fly. People gotta talk.
- Anything that can be misunderstood will be misunderstood.
- Communication is a two-way street.

What do these three statements have in common? They are the only communication concepts I recall being taught in the FBI academy. That was in the 1960s. By the 1970s greater emphasis was placed on teaching new agents the skills of properly communicating. Nevertheless these three basic communication concepts provided the fundamental building blocks for me to understand communication within the FBI. Much research in communication has occurred in the past 30 years and great strides have been made to educate the workforce throughout the criminal justice field. The use of tested communication techniques and methods has translated into greater productivity with more efficient and effective management staffs.

Communication Defined

The word communication is derived from the Latin word *communis*, meaning common. The communicator intends to establish a commonness with the receiver, therefore communication may be defined as the transmission of information and understanding through the use of common symbols.

Common symbols used by supervisors may be verbal, nonverbal, written, or a combination thereof.

Verbal symbols are words that stand for objects and abstractions. For example, if a supervisor tells a subordinate to "prepare a written report on your activities yesterday," selecting symbols (words) such as written report and activities yesterday communicate a certain expectation by the supervisor.

Nonverbal symbols are actions such as gestures, facial expressions, posture, eye contact (or lack therefore), distance, use of time, clothing, dress, appearance and voice tones. Nonverbal symbols accompany verbal symbols and are used to convey attitudes and feelings. Whenever the meaning of a nonverbal symbol conflicts with that of the verbal, the receiver is likely to find the nonverbal more believable.

Written symbols are the various forms of written communications used by supervisors to communicate with superiors and subordinates. Written communications included messages sent by facsimile machine, memos, daily reports, forms, and email.

Even private thoughts are communication. Every waking hour of our minds are full of ideas and thoughts, as many as 100,000 per day according to psychologists.

Group Discussion Questions

Communication is an art not a science. Why?

Effective supervisors are effective communicators. Why?

Is nonverbal communication more believable than verbal communication? Why?

The Communication Process

The process begins when the communicator (sender) wishes to communicate an idea or information to another person. The first step is to encode the idea or information. The sender translates information into a form that can be reduced to writing, language or nonverbal communications. Encoding can be difficult especially if the message is complex. For example, a supervisor may want a subordinate to perform a particular task in a unique manner but has difficulty explaining the request due to the subordinate's lack of experience and/or training. Without stating (encoding) the message in a manner that the subordinate can understand (decode), the supervisor has little hope of compliance with the request.

The second step in the communication process is the selection of the communication medium (channel) by the sender. The channel may be formal (official transmission of information generally in written form) or informal (generally oral communication). Once the channel is selected by the sender, the communication is sent to the intended receiver. Assuming that the message is received (which is not always the case – remember the military saying that 10% never get the word), the receiver decodes the message and provides feedback. The receiver then becomes the sender and the process continues.

In the oval below draw a picture of the communication process described above.

Effective communication must occur in a circular path.

Barriers to Effective Communication

Supervisors must communicate in a variety of situations, not all favorable to appropriate encoding and decoding. Consequently, supervisors must deal on a daily basis with many of the barriers to effective communication listed below.

- Preconceived ideas
  People hear what they want to hear (also known as selective listening).
  The eyes see and the ears hear what the mind knows (Chinese proverb).

- Denial of contrary information
  No way, I don't believe it!

- Use of personalized meanings
  Every profession has its own, unique jargon and it changes frequently.
  Example: Go down to the geedunk and get some pogey bait. This sentence is perfectly clear to a seaman – Go to the base commissary and get some candy.

- Lack of motivation or interest
  I don't have a dog in that fight, so who cares.
  Here's a quarter, so go call someone who cares.

- Use of buzz words
  Match the following words and phrases:
  1. involuntary separations   a. deaths
  2. population equivalents   b. greeting cards and gifts
  3. adverse mortality experiences c. layoffs
  4. high utilization of medical services   d. funeral homes
  5. social expression products   e. people
  6. multi-channel marketplace   f. lots of patients
  7. death care providers   g. cable television

- Non-credibility of the source
  Says who? You? I don't think so!

- Status and ability of the sender
  She's a new officer. What does she know? And she's a female.

- Lack of communication skills
  No comprende amigo. Vamonos!

Lack of education or training contributes to a subordinate's inability to understand an organization's unique language (jargon) or forms of communication (report forms and other written documents.)

- Poor organizational climate
  Sorry Sergeant, I can't talk with you about that. I'm not in your unit. See my Lieutenant.

- Stereotyping – judgments are made about communications based on the sender's traits or qualities.
  Don't pay any attention to Mack. He is KMA and hates this place.

- Communication or generation gap
  In 1995 the following words or phrases were reported by researchers to be commonly used and understood throughout the United States. How many of these words/phrases can you define?

Dropping a dime	Fink out
Slipping skin	Wasted
Tomato	Split
Platforms	Push
Bag	Dog Biscuit
Grotty	Five-percenter

In spite of the many barriers (obstacles) to effective communication, a supervisor cannot be effective as a leader, as a mentor, or as a role model for his/her employees without mastering these barriers.

Communications within Organizations

In order to be effective the first line supervisor must be aware of and participate in the flow of information within the organization. Communications typically flow in the four directions described below.

> Downward communication – flows from higher to lower levels in an organization and includes management policies, instructions, and official memos.
>
> Upward Communication – flows from lower to higher levels in an organization and includes suggestion boxes, group meetings, and grievance procedures.

Horizontal Communication – flows across functions in an organization. It is necessary for coordinating and integrating diverse organizational functions.

Diagonal Communication - cuts across functions and levels in an organization and is important in situations where members cannot communicate through upward, downward, or horizontal channels.

Basic Differences in Male/Female Communication

Communication Variable	Male	Female
Purpose for communicating	To control	To negotiate
Preferred place to communicate	Public	Private
Orientation	Competition	Cooperation
Facial Expressions	More body movements	Reveal more emotions Smiles more
Posture	Legs and arms apart More relaxed	Legs and arms together
Eye contact	Less	More
Gestures	Less	More
Use of Space	Dislikes crowding	Closer

Source: <u>You Just Don't Understand Men and Women in Conversation</u> (1990) by Deborah Tannen

In-class Group Exercise: Based on your personal and professional experiences, do you agree or disagree with Tannen's gender comparisons? Explain your answers.

Communicating with Difficult Employees

Regardless of a supervisor's communication skills and managerial abilities, problems arise between supervisors and their subordinates. Difficult employees may be viewed with the following four characterizations: whiner, bulldozer, sniper, and know-it-all. Each characterization is followed by recommended communication approaches.

Whiner – chronic complainer
> Give them recognition for what they accomplish.
> Reassure them about their abilities.
> Accept their feelings, both positive and negative.
> Check out their complaint.
> Let them vent their concerns.
> Ask them for a solution.
> Ask them how they can help make the solution happen.

Bulldozer
> Command respect. Stay in control.
> Get to the bottom line quickly.
> Focus on the issue/s, not the personality.
> Stay on track and avoid side issues.

Sniper
> Ignore sarcasm and crude humor.
> Ask for clarification – what do you mean by that?
> Do not take their remarks personal.
> Deal with issues by asking for specific information.

Know-It-All
> Turn them into mentors.

Miscellaneous Communication Concerns

Why does it really matter whether your employees like you?
> To a large extent the amount of support, commitment and cooperation that an employee gives his/her boss depends on their personal like or dislike of the individual.

How can you get others to like you? (Dale Carnegie)

Show a genuine interest in others. Smile. Use the other person's name.
Be a good listener. Make others feel important.
Talk in terms of the other person's interest.

Important common courtesies for managers:

> Say good morning and good night. Say please and thank you.
> Recognize the work of others. Use good listening skills.
> Don't use foul language, tasteless humor, put-downs or sarcasm.
> Arrive on time for meetings. Respect your employees' time.
> Don't spread or be a party to gossip.

Getting others to see your viewpoint diplomatically.

> Listen. Ask for clarification. Stay objective about what is being said.
> Decide on the validity of comments. Respond with sensitivity to the other person's position.

In-Class Exercises (Answers)

Communication or Gender Gap:
Dropping a dime (turning someone in)
Slipping skin (shaking hands)
Tomato (good looking chick)
Platforms (shoes with thick soles)
Bag (current interest)
Grotty (disgusting, nasty)
Fink out (to withdraw support from)
Wasted (penniless)
Split (leave or depart)
Push (street gang fight)
Dog Biscuit (unattractive male or female)
Five-percenter (bureaucrat on the take)

Buzz Words: 1-c, 2-e, 3-a, 4-f, 5-b, 6-g, 7-d

Sources

Bennett, Wayne W. and Karen M. Hess. <u>Management and Supervision</u>. Belmont, CA.: Wadsworth, 2001.

Carnegie, Dale. <u>How to Win Friends & Influence People</u>. New York: Pocket Books, 1936.

Gibson, James L., John M. Ivancevich and James H. Donnelly, Jr. <u>Organizations</u>. Homewood, Illinois: Business Publications, Inc., 1988.

Nichols, Michael P. <u>The Lost Art of Listening</u>. New York: Guilford Press, 1995.

Robbins, Stephen P. <u>Organizational Behavior</u>. Englewood Cliffs, NJ: Prentice Hall, 1993.

Sherman, Arthur, George Bohlander and Scott Snell. <u>Managing Human Resources</u>. Cincinnati, OH: ITP, 1996.

Problem Solving   Chapter 8

Don't tell your problems to people: eighty percent don't care; and the other twenty percent are glad you have them.   Lou Holtz

There are very few personal problems that cannot be solved through a suitable application of high explosives.   Scott Adams

Why do we need a systematic Problem-Solving Model? Why not just agree on a solution and do the job? Because today's problems are extremely complex, the answers to the problems are also complex. Having a systematic method by which complex problems may be approached and solved insures a much higher degree of success for our efforts.

Typically, there are three types of decisions that supervisors make:

- Command decisions that may only be made by the supervisor.

- Consultative decisions that are made by the supervisor after receiving input from the employees.

- Group decisions that are totally democratic in nature.

Aids to Problem Solving

- Be open to solutions: We often miss solutions by trying to control where the answers and solutions come from. Be open to solutions from any direction.

- Stay Calm: When you stay calm, you can quickly and accurately assess your situation.

- Solutions are transferable: if a problem has a solution, that solution may be transferred to solve similar problems.

- Opportunities hide in problems: solve the problem and sell the solution.

- There are usually many options: Look for them with an open mind.

- You are not alone: Others have experienced the same problem at some time in the past, so always ask for help if needed.

Problem Categories

- Tasks: A request to handle a situation. The request originates from someone other than the person completing the assignment.

    o Examples of tasks include budgets, training course certifications, and reporting procedures.

    o Three guidelines for solving tasks:
    - Insure the task is possible to achieve.

    - Make sure both parties understand the assignment by asking for and receiving feedback from the person assigned to complete the task.

    - Insure that both the individual assigning the task and the individual completing the task have agreed to undertake the task.

- Unexplained Deviations: An unexplained result in a planned action. An example would include a situation in which flyers were sent advertising a training seminar and no response was received. The common denominator with unexplained deviations generally is that the cause of the problem is unknown. The solution, therefore, is to determine the cause. In our example, one potential cause may be the flyers were not delivered to the Post Office. Another may be not enough postage, while a third may be that the Post Office failed to deliver them.

- Hurdles: Problems or Projects that are hard to perform. We encounter hurdles when we are not sure how to handle a situation, or we have insufficient resources to solve the problem. To overcome hurdles, then, we need to devote our energies to removing the blockage and/or finding the necessary resources. Hurdles can be either internal (as in lacking the skill to perform brain surgery) or external (as in solving world's hunger problem).

- Puzzles: Puzzles occur when it is known that there is a correct answer but the nature of that answer is unknown.

- o Some puzzles are solvable: The answer can be found with the information at hand.

- o Some puzzles are possibly solvable: We have some of the information but we need the rest and it is possible to get it.

- o Some puzzles are not solvable: We will probably never discover the exact route Hernando Desoto traveled in America, or the fate of Judge Crater. The solution to both of these puzzles exists but it is unlikely that we will solve either of them.

- Dilemmas: A difficult choice between two or more choices, each of which is often undesirable. With a dilemma, we may have an abundance of information but even with information, we cannot be certain that the right choice will be made. The resolution of a dilemma generally requires experience or intuitive judgment.

    - o Law enforcement officers often face dilemmas in their work. For example, in a kidnapping case, is the ransom to be paid or not? If the money is retrieved by two subjects and they split up, which one should be followed (or should either be followed because of the danger to the victim)?

    - o Assume that you are a police Chief and a small city and you have a serial murderer loose in your jurisdiction. All of your top detectives are tied up working the serial murderer case. Then you have another crisis, a workplace shooting incident. What do you do with your allocation of personnel? This is the type of dilemma all too often occurring in many jurisdictions.

- Opportunities: Overcoming a difficulty offers a potential benefit in the form of an opportunity, but it is only an opportunity if it is recognized as such. Solutions to difficult problems are often marketable. For example, it is not uncommon for law enforcement officers or prosecutors to market their experience through books, training courses and seminars.

Often the problems faced may be in more than one category. Examined the following problems and decide to which category or categories each should be assigned:

- Your supervisor asks for a report on the latest crime statistics. _____

- The State Prison Commission has to cut personnel because of budget constraints. The choices are either to cut back on the number of prison guards with longer hours for those who remain or cut salaries and hire new guards._____

- A training sergeant complains to you about the problem of constantly having to be a witness in federal civil rights cases._____

- A Police Chief gets chewed out by the Mayor and City Council because of the high number of civil rights complaints. _____

Beware of Traps

- The Forced Urgency Trap: Don't leap before you look in dealing with problems. When being pressured to handle the problem immediately, try one of the following:

    o Weigh this against other important and urgent issues and let the requester know other problems also need attention.

    o Let the person know you care but also determine the worst case scenario if it isn't handled immediately.

    o Advise the requestor that you will consider the request when you are able to set aside a sufficient block of time to examine it.

    o Put the requestor to work gathering the information you need.

- The Quick Draw: Don't jump to conclusions and look for the first easy solution. Slow down and get it right.

- The Organizational Solution: Don't always feel the way it has been done in the past is necessarily the best way. Constantly look for creative solutions for recurring problems as well as newly encountered problems.

Problem Solving Techniques

- Reality immersion: This technique allows the problem solver to gain direct experience with a situation or problem. It provides exposure of all of one's senses to the problem. Examples of reality immersion are:

    o A writer immerses himself or herself in work before writing a book to gain experience.

    o A Police Chief rides with patrol officers to get insight on how to solve a particular patrol problem.

    o An Army Officer is instructed to learn all the jobs of the enlisted personnel in the unit to determine whether they are functioning efficiently.

- Break-Out Thinking: This is thinking outside of the box, not following all the traditional assumptions, expectations or regulations. Just as a drug addict must break the addiction to function properly in society, we must occasionally break out of the institutionalized thinking to which we are often accustomed and addicted. Questions to be asked include:

    o Is there another way?

    o Can the rules be changed? Of course, this is tricky because of the need in criminal justice to stay within legal boundaries.

    o What if…?

    o Why can't we…?

The Situation Snapshot

The Situation Snapshot is a visualization of the problem or decision reduced to paper, with two columns, the left composed of supporting factors and the right composed of opposing factors. The strength of these factors is represented by strength lines. For some people, the situation snapshot helps define the problem and describes it in a visual picture.

```
                          Situation Snapshot

  Problem Description:


  Supporting Factors                              Opposing Factors
```

Gathering information

- When people approach you with problems, you needn't automatically accept their problems as your own. Ask yourself first, "Do I really want to get involved?" Here are some suggestions:

- Listen to the problem.
- Ask what they think the solution is.
- Get them to implement it.

- The above characterization is basic delegation, but beware of reverse delegation, where the employee gives the problem back to the supervisor because it is too difficult for the employee to handle.

- Ask: "Is the problem worth solving?" Often, if you ignore problems, they will disappear.

- If your problem is too large for you to handle, don't hesitate to bring in an expert.

- Subdivide the problem, if possible, into all the possible contributing factors.

- Gathering information. Information can be found from almost any source:
  - Public Sources: magazines, trade publications, government agencies, the Internet.
  - Private networking sources: training organizations, consultants, other agencies.
  - Surveys: Prosecutors, judges, defense attorneys, etc.

- Be careful, however, that you are not trying to solve the solution rather than the problem.

Group Brainstorming - Storyboarding

Brainstorming or Storyboarding is used with Consultative or Group Decisions. Those who join in should be persons affected by the decision. Stakeholders have a much higher interest level in the outcome and so are more likely to fully participate. The following are guidelines for group brainstorming:

- Ask participants to come with ideas about the subject.

- Review the rules before the session begins.

    o There should be no evaluation during the free flow of ideas.

    o Evaluation should start only after the free flow.

- Use flip charts, sticky notes or overheads. Ideally group brainstorming should have twelve people or less, located within eight to ten feet of the chart or charts.

- Visibly display the question or issue on a chart.

- Start the free flow process and aim for quantity of ideas, no matter how wild. The ideas should be added to the chart.

- Once all the ideas are listed, the evaluation process begins:

    o Most of the time you will seek good ideas with minimal investment that can be implemented immediately.

    o Many ideas you may wish to place in storage, although they are feasible.

    o In brainstorming, consensus is what is sought.

- Following the process, prepare a memo or a flow chart with the component steps and distribute it to the participants.

Storyboarding

Storyboarding is a charting method for group brainstorming. It is said to have originated by Walt Disney for use in cartoon story outlines, but has spread to the boardroom and squad room as a common technique for brainstorming. The typical storyboard looks something like the following:

STORYBOARD

Topic/Project
Date:
Project Leader:

A. Sub-Projects/Sub-Topics/Ideas/Solutions/Actions

Topics Subtopics In Top Boxes

"Other" Subtopic In Last Box

Possible Solutions

Assume you are the organization's public relations officer and in order to promote your organization, you decide to organize a 10 K race. How would you organize the race? What would your topics be and what solutions or items would be placed under them in various blocks?

STORYBOARDING

Equipment Problem

You are the Budget Administrator of a small department staffed by 12 uniformed officers, two detectives and four administrative personnel, all of whom are sworn officers. Included in the budget for the next two years is a weapons allocation of $3,800 (each year). This allocation is to pay for all weapons and to upgrade to semi-automatic pistols. Your officers carry either their own weapon with department approval or an issued .38 cal. Model 10 S&W, dated 1954 (you got a bargain on these). The department also has a total of four Remington pump shotguns, all in pretty good working order, and one AR-15 rifle that is in mint condition. Use the Storyboard with your group to break down your approach to the problem.

Training Problem

You are the chief of a small police department that has just taken on new jurisdictional territory through incorporation and will soon expand from 10 to 20 sworn officers. Your budget is tight, especially on training, but there is enough in the budget to send the 10 additional officers through POST next year. You are worried that you will not be able to adequately train your officers to meet the new POST in-service requirements (12 hours) and also provide firearms training. You are considering setting up an in-house training program where a couple of your officers get POST Certified to teach the rest of your officers in a variety of areas, including firearms. Use the Storyboard with your group to break down your approach to the problem.

Six-step problem solving mode

This method of solving problems can be used as a road map to analyze and solve individual or group problems. It works with any problem and is broken into specific steps:

- **Step One: Defining the Problem**

    o Develop a problem statement, a concise statement of the problem and brief summary of the goal.

    o It is vital to define the problem so everyone understands it. Communication is everything here.

    o The best way to avoid misunderstandings is to put it in writing.

    o Determine whether it is a Command, Consultative or Group Decision.

    o Determine what kind of problem it is: Task, Hurdle, Dilemma, etc.

    o Considerations.
        - Is it stated objectively?
        - Is it a simple statement of fact, not slanted toward any particular solution?
        - Is it limited in scope?
        - Is it achievable?
        - Does everyone involved have a common understanding of the problem?

    o Second Part of Defining the Problem: Identifying a goal or "desired state."
        - Where do you want to be when the problem is solved?
        - Example: Within six months, newly hired officers should perform at a rate of at least satisfactory on their job performance evaluations.
        - The goal should provide focus and direction.

    o Tests of a good problem statement and desired state:

- Contains ways to measure results.
- Has no implied causes.
- Has no implied solutions.
- Is short and understandable - under 15 words.

- **Step Two: Analyze Potential Causes**
    - This is the stage where questions need to be asked and information gathered, organized and analyzed.
    - There are two phases to this step:
        - First, identify all the potential causes and determine the most likely root causes of the problem.
            - Method used: Cause and effect diagram (see below).
            - Remember the Pareto Principle: 80% of the effect can usually be attributed to 20% of the cause.
        - Second, identify the true root causes.
            - Re-analyze the most likely causes to identify one or more root causes.
            - Flow charts are helpful here.

Cause and Effect Worksheet – Assistance in Finding Causes

(Also known as 3 Ms and a P)

As stated above, the cause and effect worksheet is useful to identify potential causes of a particular problem and determine the root cause. The worksheet breaks potential causes into four categories: machines, materials, methods and people. An example of a cause and effect diagram is shown below. If the coffee in the office has an off-taste, the cause of the problem may be diagnosed as follows:

Cause and Effect Worksheet

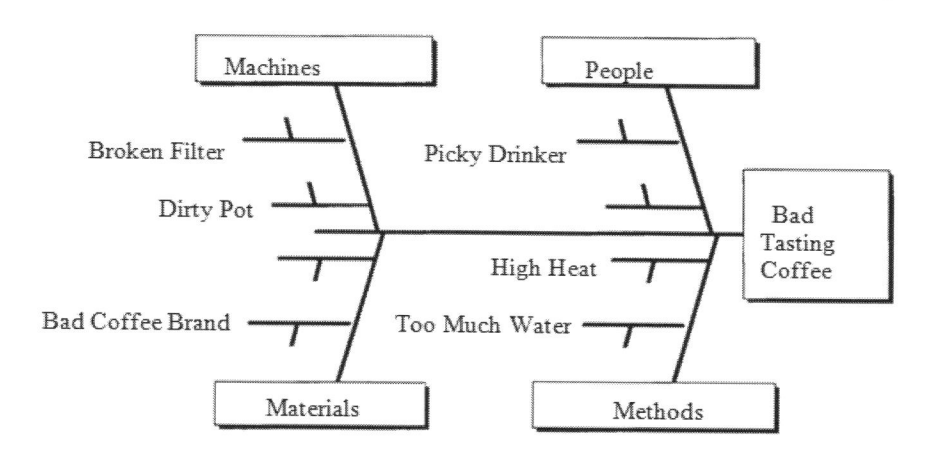

```
        Machines              People
           |                     |
  Broken Filter  \      Picky Drinker  \
                  \                     \
   Dirty Pot   \                    \         ┌──────────┐
                \                    \        │   Bad    │
                 ──────────────────────────── │ Tasting  │
                 /                   /        │  Coffee  │
                /      High Heat    /         └──────────┘
  Bad Coffee Brand /   Too Much Water /
                  /                  /
           |                     |
        Materials             Methods
```

Class Problem

As the head of the local Criminal Justice Department at Hometown University, you have been asked to write changes to your departmental policy manual because of a recurring problem involving students failing to appear in class or appearing late in class (not so many times as to be disciplined, however). The Dean has complained to you because he thinks that attending class is a low priority for your students. Using the Cause and Effect Worksheet below, determine the possible causes for the missed and late classes. Draw from your own experience the possible contributing factors leading to these.

Cause and Effect Worksheet

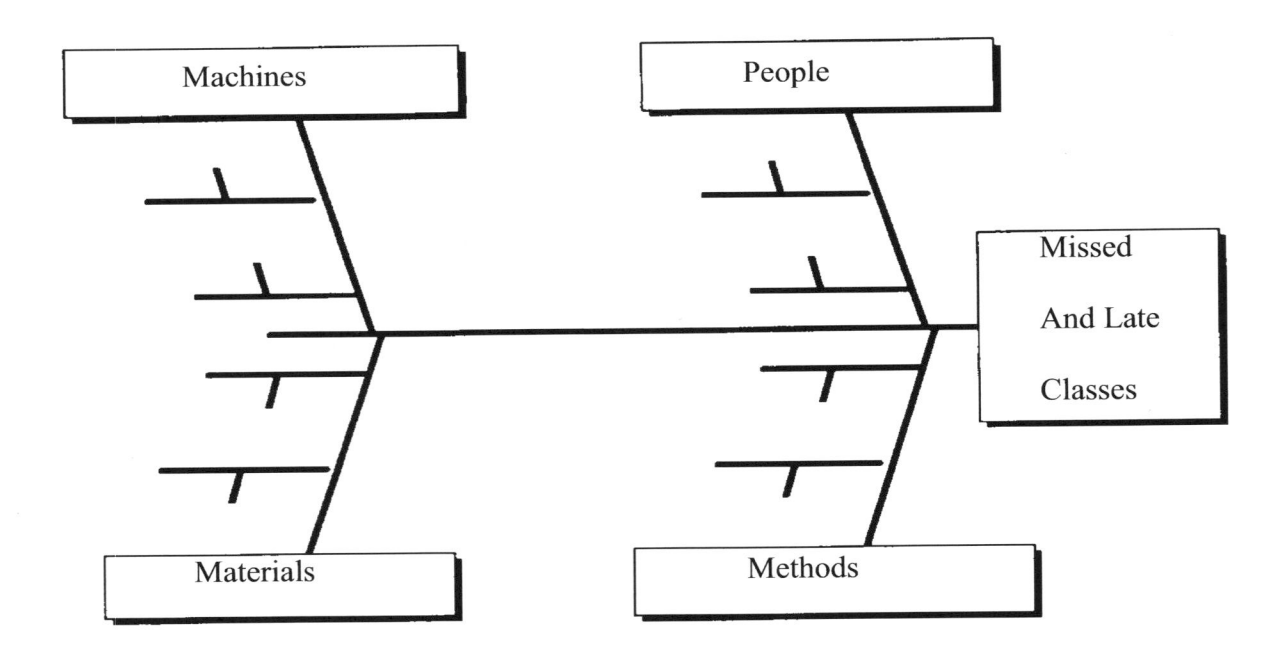

```
    Machines              People

                                              ┌─────────┐
                                              │ Missed  │
                                              │ And Late│
                                              │ Classes │
                                              └─────────┘

    Materials             Methods
```

Six-step problem solving mode (Cont.)

- **Step Three: Identify Possible Solutions**. This involves a two-step process:

  o First a list of possible solutions should be generated, taking care that no evaluation of the possible solutions is made during this process. What is needed at this time is a quantity of ideas, the more ideas the better. All possibilities should be explored and brainstorming should be the method used.

  o Next, the possible solutions are discussed and narrowed to a short list.

- **Step Four: Select the Best Solution**

    o Evaluate the possible solutions by rating them against chosen criteria (you can assign numerical weights if this is convenient).

    o There will normally be between three and six criteria involved. Possible criteria include:
    - Cost.
    - Likelihood of success.
    - Quick implementation.
    - Effectiveness.
    - Low resistance or high resistance to the implementation.

    o Rating the solutions against the criteria can be difficult if the criteria are not defined clearly.

    o The criteria must also be assigned some measure of importance such as a numerical or percentage ranking. This must be done carefully in order to insure objectivity in the process. For example, the likelihood of success may be assigned 20 percent, cost assigned 30 percent, and so on. The total should not exceed 100 percent if this is the method used.

    o Once the preliminary work has finished, the criteria should be applied to the solutions and each solution subsequently rated on a one to ten scale. The ratings score is then multiplied by the percentage assigned for the result. In this way, a best solution may be obtained without being totally subjective in the process.

- **Step Five: Develop an Action Plan**

    o An action plan is a detailed listing of action steps, personnel, start/end dates, estimated hours and costs. The action plan divides the solution into sequential tasks:
    - Action Step or Task.
    - Responsible person or group.

- Beginning Date.

- Ending Date.

- Estimated Hours to Completion.

- Cost.

The Action Plan

Action Step Task/Activity	Responsible Person/Group	Begin Date	Date	Estimated Hours	Cost

- o Other Planning Methods may be used, such as Gantt Charts, PERT Charts, and CPM (Critical Path Method) charts, as well as flow charts. The scope of these methods is beyond this study and will not be covered in this book.

- o Contingency plans should be developed according to anticipated crises. There should always be at least one alternate plan developed according to the most likely major problem anticipated.

- **Step 6: Implement the Solution and Evaluate Progress**

This ensures that the action plan is implemented and that the action steps are achieved. A monitoring system is necessary to ensure that tasks and deadlines are being met and that communication sufficient to complete the plan is present. This monitoring is normally accomplished through team meetings, briefings, and reports.

Perhaps the weakest area of criminal justice operations occurs in the evaluative stage. Usually, when some major event, operation or situation occurs, the individuals involved simply move to the next situation without detailed evaluation of what was done correctly, what was done incorrectly and what should be done prior to and during the next situation or crisis. This involves honest brainstorming, nonjudgmental critique, constructive appraisal and a willingness to change and correct established procedures.

Avoiding Traps

Ultimately, all of the above techniques could be put into place and failure may still occur, particularly if an attempt is made to solve problems that are too general, too complex or not well defined. A common mistake is to grab the first solution that seems logical without taking the time to thoroughly analyze the problem. Another fatal mistake is failure to involve stakeholders – those who are critical decision makers or employees who are directly affected by the problem, when identifying potential solutions. Finally, you must insure that the problem you are trying to solve is indeed solvable by you or your team.

Sources

Bennett, Wayne W. and Karen M. Hess. <u>Management and Supervision</u>. Belmont, CA.: Wadsworth, 2001.

Chang, Richard, and P. Keith Kelly. <u>Step-By-Step Problem Solving</u>. Irvine, CA: Richard Chang Associates, 1993.

Gibson, Bill. <u>The Art and Science of Problem Solving</u>. Niles, IL: Nightingale-Conant, 1992.

Rush, Myron. <u>Management: a Biblical Approach</u>. Wheaton, IL: Victor Books, 1983.

Budgeting Basics — Chapter 9

Here we go again – that time of year when we have the opportunity to improve our creative writing skills. Jerry Keil, Squad 4 Supervisor, Seattle FBI, 1973.

Introduction

In this chapter we will take an introductory view of budgets (a noun) and budgeting (action verb) as they apply to the first line supervisor. Most employees in criminal justice organizations are not particularly concerned with or aware of budgeting matters until they are promoted to a first line of supervision. Shortly thereafter they begin to understand why the old computers were not replaced and they are driving a vehicle with over 100,000 miles.

Preparing a budget for a security alarm company (private sector) presents fewer problems than a budget for a police department (public sector) whose services are intangible. The police department's budget is not contingent on how many arrests they make or tickets they wrote the previous year. An alarm company is profit driven – no profit, no company. This public-private sector approach to budgeting contrasts primary purposes and goals that are fundamental to an understanding of why the budget is a critical instrument in planning, administration and operations.

Definitions

The following definitions are adapted from <u>Management and Supervision</u> by Bennett and Hess and lectures by Dr. John Swain.

A *budget* is a plan or schedule adjusting expenses (costs) during a certain period to the estimated income (revenue) for that period (usually one year).

Assets are items of value owned by an agency (company).

Audit trail is the chain of references that makes it possible to trace information about transactions through an accounting system.

Contingency funds are set aside for unforeseen emergencies such as an unexpected increase in the number of prisoners housed in a county jail.

Controlling authority is the organization that gives final approval for a budget and provides guidance and oversight during the budget year to ensure compliance. At the local level for public law enforcement agencies, the controlling authority is the city council and county commission. For a private security firm, the controlling authority is the company owner or board of directors.

Expenses are the cost of providing services.

Fiscal year is the 12-month accounting period used by an agency. The period could be a calendar year or any 12 consecutive months designated by the organization.

Operating expenses are those expenses that arise from the normal activities of the organization.

Variable costs are costs that vary in total directly with the amount of service provided, i.e., personnel costs including overtime.

Types of Budgets

While criminal justice organizations in the public and private sectors do not use the same type of budget, most organizations have an operating budget and a capital budget. Some organizations have a third type of budget, a discretionary budget. These types of budgets are defined and examples provided.

Operating Budget – deals with all expenses needed to run (operate) an organization. These expenses may include salaries and equipment needed to meet the goals of the organization. Some agencies deal with personnel costs as a separate expense although it is generally included as a significant part of the operating budget (75-80%).

Capital Budget – capital expenses are expensive items that are essential to the operation of the organization such as buildings, vehicles, and computers. Some organizations define a capital expense as any item costing more than $100 and will be used for more than one year. These items are depreciated over a period a time, and usually replaced.

Discretionary Budget – monies that are set aside for use as needed. These items are not specifically budgeted but may be acquired as management deems appropriate.

Purpose of a Budget

Budgets serve as a plan for and a means to control resources. Individuals control their spending by living within their means and the budget provides the accounting tool. Similarly, budgets are used by supervisors to monitor spending and make monthly adjustments so that the organization does not run out of money before the end of the year. Budgeting is a continuous process not just a once-a-year concern at "budget time."

Responsibility for Budget Preparation

Criminal justice organizations approach budget preparation differently depending on the style of management by the chief executive officer and guidelines set by the controlling authority. Budget preparation may be the responsibility of a separate division (large organizations), finance department, budget committee (usually three or more employees including senior managers) or one designated employee. In smaller organizations budgets are prepared by the chief executive officer, such as the chief of police, sheriff of a small county, the district attorney, or the warden of a small jail. Even though the ultimate responsibility for budget preparation rests with the chief executive officer, most lower levels of supervision become involved in the collection of data and provide estimates of future needs for services and expenses. Preparing a budget is making estimates of future needs.

The Budget Process

The budget process follows a systematic procedure that typically involves some variation of the following steps:

- The controlling authority (such as the city council or the county commission) initiates the annual budget process (the Call) by notifying all participants of what is needed and a schedule for submitting the data. A copy of last year's budget is attached to the Call for guidance in making future estimates.

- Supervisors of the various departments and units begin collecting data by reviewing expenses for the past year, noting categories of expenses that were depleted before the end of the year and categories of spending that fell short of the projected costs.

Supervisors may solicit input from unit members and actively involve them in preparing the unit budget.

- These unit projections are sent up the chain of command and eventually arrive on the desk of the chief executive officer. The CEO has the ultimate responsibility for submitting the budget to the controlling authority. The CEO may hold budget meetings with department heads to clarify estimates and prepare for his/her budget presentation.

- On a designated date (identified in the Call), the CEO or someone from the organization acting on his/her behalf presents the budget to the controlling authority.

- The controlling authority reviews each item in the budget and decides whether or not 1) the projections (requested funds) are realistic and 2) projected revenue will cover these expenses.
- Following negotiations and further meetings between the controlling authority and the CEO, a budget for the organization is approved and disseminated to managers who are charged with the responsibility of monitoring monthly expenses.

- Records are maintained and closely monitored during the year as the process continues year after year.

Budget Systems

One or more of the following budget systems may be found in criminal justice organizations. In some instances organizations use a combination of these systems.

Lump Sum Budget

A lump sum budget is the simplest budget and sets forth one amount for each organization under its authority. This budget does not address how monies are to be spent and leaves the details to the CEOs. Each department is allocated a specific amount of money to spend within the fiscal year. Department heads are responsible for monitoring expenses to ensure that each unit does not exceed the total amount allocated for the fiscal year. Here is an example:

Snake Navel, Idaho ~ FY 2001 Budgets	
Police Department	199,000
Fire Department	21,000
Street Department	11,000
Elected Official Salaries	8,000
	239,000

Line Item Budget

The line item budget emerged in the early 1900s and is one of the most common budgets used by criminal justice organizations regardless of size. This type of budget is like a grocery list, specific expenses (line items) are identified and dollars allocated (Swain). Line item budgets are usually based on the preceding year's budget with a comparison between the budgeted amount and the actual expense. Here is an example:

Snake Navel, Idaho Police Department ~ FY 2001	
Personnel	143,000
Chief 30,000; Lieutenant 20,000; eight patrol officers @10,000 each; overtime – 10% of annual pay	
Vehicles (Two vehicles @ 15,000 each)	30,000
Vehicle Supplies (Gasoline 13,000; Misc. 2,000)	15,000
Gasoline 13,000; Misc. 2,000	
Vehicle Maintenance	4,000
Equipment	3,000
Training	2,000
Station Supplies	1,000
Telephone	1,000
	199,000

Performance Budgeting

Performance based budgeting allocates dollars based on productivity. For a large law office the civil division might bring in more money than the criminal division. Therefore, more money will be budgeted to support their activities. In a sheriff's department, the civil division (responsible for serving subpoenas) is compared with the criminal division and jail division in terms of what services they provide and the cost of each service. Here is an example of a performance budget for the patrol division of a police department:

Snake Navel, Idaho Police Department (SNPD)
FY 2001

Performance Activity: Patrol
Unit: man-vehicle hours
13,140 units per year

The SNPD patrol policy is one officer per vehicle for 36 hours of patrol a day.

Line Items

Personnel (Six patrol officers at 20,000 each)............	**120,000**
Vehicles (One new vehicle per year)	15,000
Vehicle supplies	15,000
Vehicle maintenance	5,000
Equipment	1,000
	156,000

Unit cost: $11.87 per man-vehicle hour of patrol

Program Budgeting

This form of budgeting identifies the various programs (services) that an organization provides and allocates monies for each. A percentage of administrative costs, support costs, and overhead expenses (operating expenses) are assigned to each program. This approach is manpower intense, requiring a great deal of paperwork generated by trained personnel. Program budgeting allows CEOs to quickly identify program cuts during periods of downsizing due to shortfalls in revenue. Here is an example:

Snake Navel, Idaho Police Department
FY 2001

Program: Crime Solution
Program Costs: 48,500

Line Items

Personnel		41,000
10% of Chief's Time	3,000	
20% of Lieutenant's Time	4,000	
Two detectives at $15,000 each	30,000	
Vehicles (50% of vehicles)		3,500
Vehicle Supplies and Maintenance		3,000
Supplies		1,000
Telephone		1,000

Performance Data-Projected Activities

Index Crimes Investigated		Number Cleared	Solution Rate
Murder	1	1	100%
Forcible Rape	1	1	100
Robbery	3	2	66.6
Aggravated Assault	10	6	60
Burglary	25	7	28
Larceny-Theft	95	25	26
Motor Vehicle Theft	10	2	20

Zero-Based Budgeting (ZBB)

ZBB received national attention when Jimmy Carter, former Governor of Georgia, was elected president in 1977 and introduced ZBB which had been successfully used in the state of Georgia. This system of budgeting begins anew each budget year and requires justification of all expenses regardless of expenses the prior fiscal year. All budget lines begin at zero and are funded according to merit rather than in accordance with the preceding year. The controlling authority reviews requests for funds, identifies objectives and compares these objectives with competing programs. The system is intended to cut waste, stop duplication and require organizations to justify all expenses, even personnel. Swain argues that ZBB is not needed every year but may be useful every 5 to 10 years for most organizations. Here is an example:

Snake Navel, Idaho   FY 2001
Police Department   Decision Unit: Patrol
Decision Package 1 of 3: Patrol   Cost: 88,000
Activity: 36 hours daily of one-man per vehicle   Cumulative Cost: 88,000

Line Items
Personnel ……………………………………………………………………… 60,000
Vehicles ……………………………………………………………………… **27,000**
Miscellaneous …………………………………………………………………   1,000
                                                                      88,000

Decision Package 2 of 3: Patrol   Cost: 21,000
Activity: 12 additional hours daily vehicle patrol   Cumulative Cost: 109,000

Line Items
Personnel ……………………………………………………………………… 15,000
Vehicle …………………………………………………………………………   5,000
Miscellaneous …………………………………………………………………   1,000

Decision Package 3 of 3: Patrol Cost: 25,000
Activity: 12 man hours daily foot patrol Cumulative Cost: 134,000
Cumulative level of activities: 48 hours of vehicle patrol and 12 hours of daily foot patrol

Line Items
Personnel 22,000
Equipment .... <u>3,000</u>
                                                                                   25,000

Summary

In this chapter we have attempted to answer the question, why are budget and budgeting important for first line supervisors. Relevant terms have been defined and a brief view of the budgeting process and certain budgeting systems were presented. Students are reminded that criminal justice organizations do not adhere precisely to the systems and process discussed herein. Most organizations use some elements of each budget type to meet their particular needs. Nevertheless the concepts presented in this chapter should provide criminal justice students with a general understanding of budgets and budgeting.

In-Class Group Exercise

As a new lieutenant in the Snake Navel, Idaho Police Department (SNPD), you have just been placed in charge of a new unit – the gang suppression unit. Gang activity has increased in recent months at the local high school resulting in assaults, robbery, theft, and one death. The chief of the SNPD wants you to prepare a one-year budget based on your estimated needs for personnel (officers) and equipment to carry out this assignment. Based on information and examples provided in this chapter, prepare two budgets (line item and performance) for this police service.

Sources

Bennett, Wayne and Karen M. Hess. <u>Management and Supervision</u>. Belmont, CA: Wadsworth, 2001.

Cordner, Gary W. and Robert Sheehan. <u>Police Administration</u>. Cincinnati, OH: Anderson, 1999.

Harris, Louis M., Jr. <u>Zero-Based Budgeting</u>. A paper prepared for PSC 667, Public Budgeting, Instructor – Dr. John Swain, The University of Alabama. 24 Oct 1994.

Peak, Kenneth J. <u>Justice Administration</u>. Englewood, NJ: Prentice Hall, 1995.

Swain, John. <u>Lectures in Public Budgeting</u>, PSC 667. The University of Alabama. Fall 1994.

Stress Management — Chapter 10

Cast your cares on the Lord, and he will sustain you. Psalm 55:22

Ulcers? I give 'em. I don't get 'em. Anonymous CEO

Introduction

Stress may be viewed by a supervisor from three perspectives: the individual (supervisor), the work group (the supervisor's subordinates), and the organization (the agency that employs the supervisor). This chapter will consider stress and stress management from all three perspectives. You will also be given several widely used self-assessment stress tests to measure your current stress levels and create a greater awareness of stress levels in the workplace.

As you begin this chapter, try to answer these questions:

- Why is it important for supervisors to understand stress and stress management?

- How stressful are CJ jobs?

If you have an understanding of the concepts in these questions and their application to your workplace, you will appreciate the stress perspectives presented in this chapter. If you are not familiar with these concepts, this chapter will introduce you to stress concepts and stress management as they apply to the criminal justice field.

Ways of Defining Stress

Stress may be defined as …

> Anything a person perceives as an overload; too big, too soon, too often, too hard or too much.

> Any adjustment demand caused by physical, mental or emotional factors that requires coping behavior (Sherman et al 488).

A dynamic condition in which an individual is confronted with an opportunity, constrain, or demand related to what he or she desires and for which the outcome is perceived to be both uncertain and important (Robbins 635).

Stress may be positive (eustress) or negative (distress).

Eustress occurs from positive events such as receiving raises; it is the stress of meeting challenges (Leap and Crino 542).

Distress is harmful stress that is characterized by a loss of feelings of security and adequacy (Sherman et al 488).

Stress Test – Part 1

Read and choose the most appropriate answer for each of the 10 questions as it actually pertains to you. Place the appropriate letter in the space before each question.

        A = Almost always true
        B = Usually true
        C = Usually false
        D = Almost always false

_____ 1. When I can't do something "my way," I simply adjust to do it the easiest way.
_____ 2. I get "upset" when someone in front of me drives slowly.
_____ 3. It bothers me when my plans are dependent upon others.
_____ 4. Whenever possible, I tend to avoid large crowds.
_____ 5. I am uncomfortable having to stand in long lines.
_____ 6. Arguments upset me.
_____ 7. When my plans don't flow smoothly, I become anxious.
_____ 8. I require a lot of room (space) to live and work in.
_____ 9. When I am busy at some task, I hate to be disturbed.
_____ 10. I believe that all good things are worth waiting for.

To Score: Questions 1 and 10   A = 1 pt. B = 2 pts. C = 3 pts. D = 4 pts.
           Questions 2 thru 9   A = 4 pts B = 3 pts. C = 2 pts. D = 1 pt.

This test measures your vulnerability to stress from being frustrated, i.e., inhibited. Scores in excess of 25 suggest some vulnerability to this source of stress.

Categories of Stress ~~ Frustrations ~~ Conflicts ~~ Pressures

Frustrations are obstacles that block progress toward a goal. Frustrations may be caused by a lack of education, prejudice, discrimination, lack of opportunity, lack of motivation, personal limitations, and the glass ceiling.

Conflicts occur when choices are made to satisfy needs. Stress occurs when an employee is offered a promotion that will require a transfer to a different state. The employee believes that the promotion will enhance his/her career and earn more money but the move will be devastating to his/her family, particularly teenage children.

Pressures occur when an effort is made by an organization to require that employees achieve certain goals or behave in a certain manner. Some common areas of pressures exerted by organizations involve enforcing a dress code, monitoring punctuality, enforcing standards of personal conduct on and off the job, and demanding loyalty to the organization.

Sources of Stress ~~ External ~~ Internal

Common External Stressors in the CJ Environment
    Frustration with the CJ System
    Lack of consideration in scheduling employees for court appearances
        Perception of inadequate public support
    Perception of negative public attitudes
    Negative, biased, and inaccurate media coverage

Common Internal Stressors in the CJ Environment
    Policies and procedures which employees do not support
    Inadequate training; inadequate career development
    Inadequate recognition and rewards for good work
    Inadequate salary, benefits and working conditions
    Inconsistent discipline; favoritism regarding promotions and assignments
    Politically motivated administrative decisions

General Criminal Justice Environment Stressors
    Unhealthy consequences of shift work
    Potential role conflict between the mission and serving the public
    Frequent exposure to human suffering
    Boredom interrupted by the need for sudden alertness

Fear and danger involved in certain situations
Being responsible for protecting other people
Too much work to do in time allotted
Fears regarding job competence and success
Fears regarding personal safety
The possible need to take other jobs to support family
Need for further education
Altered social status in the community

In-Class Group Exercise: Form discussion groups made up of common jobs and prepare a list of common external and external stressors in your profession. Students who are not currently working in the criminal justice field should join a group that represents their career goals.

Internal Stressors

_____   _____

_____   _____

External Stressors

_____   _____

_____   _____

Factors influencing the severity of stress

Nature of the stressor
    Importance – life or death to no importance
    Duration
        Short duration – can usually be handled easily
        Long duration – must having coping techniques to survive

Cumulating Effect
> The last straw analogy

Multiplicity
> Many stressors at once

Imminence
> Dreading the inevitable

Individual stress tolerance
> Each person brings a unique mix of personality traits and characteristics to the workplace. These factors may be categorized as personality types.

> Type A – obsessed with a sense of urgency, try to do several things at once, hostile, impatient, speaks in staccato, tends to finish another's sentences, competitive, difficult to work with, and drives themselves harder than subordinates.

> Type B – rarely driven to increase quantity of work, focus on quality of work, focus on quality of life, and as intelligent, ambitious and successful as Type A.

> Type C – the "nice guy" who wants to please others even to his own detriment; holds in own needs, frustrations and anger; cover up for lack of self esteem; almost never vents anger, sadness, or fear; has negative feelings but does not express them.

> Type H – hostility personality: Take the following quiz to determine if you have any of the Type H characteristics:

> 1 – Do you think you have to yell at subordinates so they don't mess up or to get their attention?
> 2 – Do you assume cashiers will shortchange you if they can?
> 3 – If your child spills milk, do you immediately yell?
> 4 – After an irritating encounter, do you feel shaky or breathless?
> 5 – Do you feel your anger is justified and feel an urge to punish people?
> 6 – Do you get angry every time you stand in line or get behind the wheel?

> What to do to combat Type H personality:

> 1 – Face up to it. Recognize that you may have a hostile personality at times.

2 – Just say "stop." Decide to do something about it by telling someone who can hold you accountable.
3 – Put yourself in another person's shoes. Try to understand the other person's perspective.
4 – Practice relaxation techniques. Take several deep breaths. Think about something pleasant.
5 – Don't sit and steam. Change your environment. Let it go. Get over it.
6 – Forgive and forget. Move on with your life.

External resources and social supports
Family, friends, co-workers, confidants, professional groups, and religious supports

Stress Test – Part Two

Circle the letter of the response option that best answers the following 10 questions.
A = Almost always   B = Very often   C = Seldom   D = Never

How often do you …
A B C D 1. Find yourself with insufficient time to complete your work?
A B C D 2. Find yourself becoming confused and unable to think clearly because too many things are happening at once?
A B C D 3. Wish you had help to get everything done?
A B C D 4. Feel you boss simply expects too much from you?
A B C D 5. Feel your family/friends expect too much from you?
A B C D 6. Find your work infringing upon your leisure time?
A B C D 7. Find yourself doing extra work to set an example to those around you?
A B C D 8. Find yourself doing extra work to impress your superiors?
A B C D 9. Have to skip a meal so that you can get work completed?
A B C D 10. Feel that you have too much responsibility?

To Score: A = 4 pts.   B = 3 pts.   C = 2 pts.   D = 1 pt.

This test measures you vulnerability to overload, i.e., having too much to do.
Scores in excess of 25 indicate vulnerability to this source of stress.

Predictors of Stress

Stages of Stress Development: Primary, Advance and Severe
> Primary signs of stress
>> Clenched teeth, tight muscles, curled toes, neck pain, rapid and shallow breathing, perspiration, rapid pulse, and hand temperature cooler than neck
>
> Advanced signs of stress
>> Irritability, headaches, backaches, bowel problems, depression, apathy, sleeping problems, increase in smoking/drinking and loss interest in sex
>
> Severe signs of stress
>> Asthma, hypertension, heart disease, ulcers and cancer

Physical Symptoms of Stress
> Feeling exhausted and fatigued; having a lingering cold; having frequent headaches; gastro-intestinal disorders; being unable to sleep; shortness of breath; sudden gain/loss in body weight; increased blood pressure; and, increased susceptibility to illness.

Psychological Symptoms of Stress
> Thinking becomes rigid and inflexible; feeling of "knowing it all"; resists change, even if change may be positive; bad attitude; feelings of hopelessness; feelings of helplessness; depression; guilt feelings for not doing enough; suspicion and paranoia; unreliable judgment and reasoning; withdrawal from job and home; and over confidence.

Stress and Burn-out

Individuals with the following characteristics are likely candidates for burn-out:
- Those who are not suited for the work to which they are assigned;
- Those who are bored or locked into a routine;
- Those who work in a highly stressful environment, especially if it is emotionally charged over an extended period of time;
- Those in daily contact with the public because of the necessity to adapt rapidly to different people and/or situations; and
- Those who are dedicated and committed.

Characteristics of Stress-Resistant Supervisors

The following characteristics typify supervisors who effectively deal with stress:

- In control of self
- Deeply committed to the work
- Deeply committed to their own values
- Treat demands as challenges

Managing Personal Stress

Personal health standards

    Exercise frequently. Do something that gets your heart rate up to at least 75% of its maximum three to four times a week. Maintain your ideal weight. Eat breakfast. Do not skip meals. Get seven to eight hours of sleep a night. Do not use tobacco and little to no caffeine. Establish and maintain a belief system.

Coping behaviors

    Clarify your values. Improve self talks. Learn how to relax. Exercise regularly. Get the leisure you need. Adopt dietary goals. Avoid the chemical haze.

Stress accumulation avoidance

    Avoid dependencies. Practice belly breathing. Relax muscles. Exercise. Look out the window for a diversion. Don't answer the phone on the first ring. Don't make mountains out of molehills. Replay good times in your mind. Manage your time better. Learn to say no. Escape or avoid stressful situations. Grin and bear it. Take life one day at a time. Take life as it comes.

Stress Test – Part 3
Answer all questions as is generally true for you. Place the appropriate letter in the space before each question.
A = Almost always true   B = Usually true   C = Seldom true   D = Never true

_____ 1. I hate to wait in lines.
_____ 2. I often find myself racing against the clock to save time.
_____ 3. I become upset if I think something is taking too long.
_____ 4. When under pressure, I tend to lost my temper.
_____ 5. My friends tell me that I tend to get irritated easily.
_____ 6. I seldom like to do anything unless I can make it competitive.
_____ 7. When something needs to be done, I'm the first to begin even though the details may still need to be worked out.
_____ 8. When I make a mistake, it is usually because I've rushed into something

without giving it enough thought and planning.

_____ 9. Whenever possible, I will try to do two things at once, like eating while working, or planning while driving or bathing.

_____ 10. When I go on a vacation, I usually take some work along just in case I get a chance.

To Score: A = 4 pts.   B = 3 pts.   C = 2 pts.   D = 1 pt.

This test measures the presence of compulsive, time urgent, and excessively aggressive behavioral trains. Scores in excess of 25 suggest the presence of one or more of these traits.

Managing Employee Stress

Improve management skills
    Discuss stress management with subordinates.
    Provide stress training for subordinates.

Improve organization communication
    Identify communication problems that create stress and work to eliminate them.
    Be aware of internal and external problems that can be improved.
    Increase formal communication with subordinates to reduce uncertainty.

Improve workplace environment
    Upgrade the quality of equipment whenever possible.
    Provide the best workspace possible to meet employee needs.

Establish physical fitness programs (wellness programs)
    Provide a workout space (room) for employees to use before or after work.
    Encourage employees to work out at least three times a week.
    Provide information to employees on health standards and dietary control.
    Conduct periodic self-assessments of fitness.

Plan family activities
    Schedule quarterly social events for employees and their families.
    Hold periodic staff-spouse meetings to inform spouses of workplace issues.

Establish peer-counseling programs
    Match new employees with experienced employees to provide mentoring.
    Recognize individual needs and refer for counseling as appropriate.

Summary and Conclusions

What is a *good place to work*? In a survey of over 100 organizations, five phrases were repeatedly used to answer this question (Levering 336). Here they are:

This is a friendly place.
There isn't much politicking around here.
You get a fair shake in this organization.
This is more than a job.
It's just like a family around here.

How does this list compare with what you think makes up a good place to work? Create your own list here.

Sources

Carrell, Michael R., Frank E. Kuzmits and Norbert F. Elbert. <u>Personnel/Human Resource Management</u>. New York: Macmillan Publishing, 1992.

Leap, Terry L. and Michael D. Crino. <u>Personnel/Human Resource Management</u>. New York: Macmillan Publishing, 1993.

Levering, R. <u>A Great Place to Work</u>. New York: Random House, 1988.

Morris, Charles G. <u>Psychology</u>. Englewood Cliffs, NJ: Prentice Hall, 1985.

Robbins, Stephen P. <u>Organizational Behavior</u>. Englewood Cliffs, NJ: Prentice Hall, 1993.

Sherman, Arthur, George Bohlander, and Scott Snell. <u>Managing Human Resources</u>. Cincinnati, OH: ITP, 1996.

Conflict Resolution   Chapter 11

Conflict is inevitable, but combat is optional.   Max Lucado

The quality of our lives depends not on whether or not we have conflicts, but on how we respond to them.   Tom Crum

Conflict Resolution, also known as Alternative Dispute Resolution (ADR), has many forms and hybrid variations. The two most common forms are mediation and arbitration. All of these deal with conflict, a difference in opinion or purpose that frustrates someone's goals or desires. Conflict is inevitable in life and should be expected in the workplace as well as in life. How supervisors respond to conflict will contribute to a large extent to their success or failure as a leader.

Also, despite what is commonly thought, conflict is not always bad if lessons are learned and subsequently applied or if growth ensues. The causes of conflict include the following:

- Misunderstandings.

- Differences.

- Competition.

- Selfish attitudes and desires.

At one end of the spectrum, conflict produces escape responses such as denial that a problem exists, flight from the problem in order to avoid its consequences, or in the most extreme of cases, suicide. At the opposite extreme are attack responses such as litigation, assault and ultimately, murder.

Between these two extremes are the alternative dispute responses:

- Negotiation.

- Mediation.

- Arbitration.

We will cover negotiation in a separate chapter because of its scope; however, it should be noted that negotiation is used as a communication tool in both mediation and arbitration.

Mediation

Mediation is generally considered to be the purest form of alternative dispute resolution. In application, it attempts to be a win-win solution and often succeeds. One of the advantages of mediation is that it is totally informal and can be accomplished at any place or time. Mediators frequently use courtrooms, Bar Association offices, motel rooms, telephones and automobiles during their mediation sessions. Another advantage is that it is inexpensive when compared with litigating a dispute. Mediators often charge between $25 and $250 per hour, depending upon the type of case and the experience of the mediator. Some mediation contracts pay by the case instead of the hour. At the current time, the United States government contracts for mediation pay between $500 and $2,000 per case for employment discrimination claims. Studies have shown that the average mediation session runs between four and six hours in length.

Because the process is informal and is guided by the parties themselves, no agreement is binding unless it is reached by the parties and reduced to writing. Once it has taken on written form, it becomes a binding contract or agreement and is therefore legally enforceable. Another advantage from the mediator's point of view is that the proceedings are considered confidential in nature. Because of the confidentiality, the information learned may not be used by either party to gain an advantage in a later trial. Further, mediators, according to state and federal law, are prohibited from testifying in trials arising out of mediations. This protects the process and the individuals involved and promotes a free flow of ideas during the sessions.

Because of the above described advantages, mediation enjoys a relatively high success rate nationally, currently being slightly over sixty percent. The U.S. Postal Service even claims an eighty-two percent success rate for its year 2009 employment mediation program.

Mediation can be used in virtually any situation, from hostage negotiation and victim/witness-perpetrator conciliation to divorce situations. Employment mediation is used extensively by federal agencies, including the Federal Bureau of Investigation, which implemented an ADR program in the late 1980s. This program continues today and is greatly supported by all ranks of the organization.

Mediation so far has not been implemented to any great extent in local or state organizations, including law enforcement organizations. Because of the success rate and because of the time and money saved, however, departments are increasingly examining mediation programs for adoption.

Why would law enforcement administrators be reluctant to implement such a program?

Despite the fact that no formal program may exist in your organization, supervisors will inevitably mediate disputes between employees or between groups of employees. Mediation skills can be learned through formal training but are best utilized through experience. For mediation to have any chance of success, supervisors must be viewed by the parties involved as impartial during the dispute.

Arbitration

Arbitration is a process in which an arbitrator or panel of arbitrators hears an abbreviated summary of the evidence in a conflict and then renders an award after determining liability and damages. The evidence in arbitration cases is usually submitted in narrative form; that is, without examination and cross examination according to the established rules of courtroom conduct. If so stipulated by the parties, arbitration is binding. The process of arbitration itself benefits the parties in concept because of the savings they reap by not having to go through the costly process of a trial. Supervisors often act as arbitrators within their areas of influence, and frequently an outside arbitrator (chief law enforcement officer) intervenes to decide a dispute.

Businesses contend that the cost of litigation and the tendency of juries in recent years to order extravagant judgments based largely upon emotion have forced them to turn to arbitration for protection. In their view the legal system, aided by the government, has produced a legal lottery in which anyone can claim victim status against business and industry, which are perceived as having unlimited funds to pay to pay for claimed wrongs despite the lack of provable injury. Companies have therefore turned to arbitration for protection.

In actual fact, arbitration may not provide a fair adjudication in all circumstances due to the often imposed requirement that the parties submit their case to a particular group of arbitrators (chosen by the company), when in fact the arbitration group may have a close working or business arrangement with the company. The system would be more fairly applied if each side were allowed to choose a particular arbitrator and the chosen arbitrators selected a third arbitrator to work with them. The system then would not benefit one-party over the other.

Other Forms of ADR

- Mini Trials involve having currently sitting (or retired Judges) who hear an abbreviated version of the evidence and issue a non-binding opinion on liability, damages or both. This gives the attorneys for both sides the ability to show their clients what would probably happen in court if the case were tried. The theory is that cases would settle quicker and at less expense if the clients understood the likely outcome. In fact, Mini Trials are not used frequently today, but the idea may be accepted to a greater extent in the future, particularly as litigation expenses and awards increase.

- Med-Arb is a hybrid process which combines mediation and arbitration. First, there is an attempt to mediate the dispute through a "neutral," but if mediation is unsuccessful, the neutral becomes an arbitrator. The arbitration can be binding or non-binding (reserving the right to sue under certain conditions), while another option refers the dispute to an arbitration panel if the mediation is unsuccessful.

Preparing to Mediate

Many mediators use some form of systematic format in order to prepare for a mediation. The following system, the PAUSE Principle, is representative of this type of format:

- **P**repare. Prior to entering into any mediation, the mediator should attempt to gain as much knowledge about the situation as possible. It is usually very helpful to know what the facts and issues are before beginning the process. Ironically, some organizations prefer that the mediator enter the process with no advanced knowledge other than an overall understanding of the nature of the dispute, such as employment, divorce, fee collection or similar topic. The rationale behind this is to prevent the mediator from becoming biased toward either side.

    What would be the downside to this approach?

- **A**ffirm Relationships. The beginning of any mediation should be devoted to putting the parties at ease and attempting to establish an affinity with them. Mediators must be trusted and have to earn this trust in the first ten or fifteen minutes of the process.

- Understand Interests. The next step, and perhaps the most difficult, is to separate interests from positions. A position is that which is stated by a party to represent what he or she wants. An interest, on the other hand, is what he or she actually desires from the mediation. A person's interest and position may be entirely different and it is the mediator's job to differentiate between the two by asking probing questions and carefully listing to the answers given. Once an understanding of interests is reached by the mediator, the process can move forward by seeking solutions.

- Search for Creative Solutions. This is the most interesting and rewarding part of the mediation. In this phase, skillful mediators can coax alternative solutions to the dispute from both sides, with the mediator also throwing in a few. The process at this point closely resembles brainstorming, with liberal use of charts and storyboards.

- Evaluate Options. Again, like brainstorming, listed options are examined and evaluated by all parties until the most satisfactory option is chosen. The mediator seeks to separate the people from the problem at this stage so that they are jointly evaluating a problem dispassionately and seeking a common solution.

The Mediator's Monologue

In beginning the process, the mediator usually opens with a monologue which contains one or more of the following points:

- The Introduction, where the mediator reviews his or her credentials. Obviously, this can be omitted when the mediator is also a supervisor or is otherwise known to the parties.

- The Process of mediation is explained to the parties.

- The use of Caucuses is reviewed. A caucus is a private meeting between the mediator and each party. The mediator may ask for a caucus at any time and either party may ask for a caucus. Caucuses are used to openly explain a position, explore possibilities for settlement and to assure the party that the mediator will reveal from the caucus only that information which is authorized by the party during the caucus.

- Confidentiality Rules. The mediator should advise both parties that the information revealed by either side during the mediation is protected under state and federal law from being used to gain an advantage for litigation. Further, it is explained that the mediator may not be subpoenaed by either party to testify at a trial or hearing, and that the mediator's notes will be destroyed shortly after the mediation.

    Why would a mediator advise the parties that mediation notes will be destroyed?

- Review Other Rules which the parties may decide to enforce, such as which party will speak first and whether or not to allow interruptions during the speech. Often, one or more parties are represented by attorneys. If so, the mediator must determine whether the party or the attorney will speak. Other rules may be adopted depending upon the issue and situation.

Once the ground rules have been agreed upon, the final stage in the monologue is usually to seek a commitment from each party to begin the mediation process.

During the process itself, one side (normally the party making the complaint) will usually be asked to speak and outline a position without interruption by the opposing party. The situation is then reversed, with the opposing party being asked to speak about the dispute (with no interruption by the complaining party). The mediator may ask for a caucus at this time where the parties can speak freely about their weak points, strong points and options. Some mediators attempt to push parties in caucuses so that they will be willing to compromise or at least look at the dispute more realistically, having heard the other side's position. Other mediators allow the parties to arrive at their own agreement by skillfully drawing out each side's interest, thereby encouraging the parties to reach an agreement that benefits both sides.

If the parties are not that far apart to begin with, the mediator may forgo a caucus so that the parties may talk the problem through to a logical conclusion. Mediators must be willing to examine an issue from a number of different views and must also exhibit infinite patience when dealing with disputants. Successful mediators understand that tensions are often high, especially at the outset of a mediation, and must be prepared to use every method available to calm the parties when tempers flare.

A diligent mediator may expect to settle the majority of cases encountered no matter what the issue. For this reason, mediation in criminal justice has a bright future and is just beginning to change the workplace. For law enforcement, mediation techniques work as well in street encounters as they do in judicial settings. Officers, corrections personnel, administrators and private industry supervisors will all benefit from understanding the process of mediation and applying mediation principles to everyday life at home, in the office and on the street.

Sources

Baruch Bush, Robert A., and Joseph P. Folger. The Promise of Mediation. San Francisco: Jossey-Bass, 1994.

Beer, Jennifer E. The Mediator's Handbook. Gabriola Island, BC: New Society Publishers, 1997.

Constantino, Cathy A., and Christina Sickles Merchant. Designing Conflict Management Systems. San Francisco: Jossey-Bass, 1996.

Galton, Eric. Representing Clients in Mediation. Dallas, TX: Texas Lawyer Press, 1994.

Sande, Ken. The Peacemaker. Grand Rapids, MI: Baker Book House, 1991.

Practical Negotiation   **Chapter 12**

Man is an animal that makes bargains: no other animal does this - no dog exchanges bones with another.   Adam Smith

The most difficult thing in any negotiation, almost, is making sure that you strip it of the emotion and deal with the facts.   Howard Baker

---

Most people go through life never realizing that they negotiate things on a daily basis. Some things they negotiate well and some poorly, but negotiations continue day after day from childhood to death. Understanding how negotiation works and how people respond to offers of negotiation will certainly improve the ability of the average person to successfully negotiate at home and at work.

There are three components of every negotiation – power, information and time. Each of these will be discussed in this chapter along with tactics for using them advantageously during negotiation sessions.

Another underlying principle for every negotiation is the need to structure the negotiation so that a Win/Win situation occurs. This means that every party in the negotiation must win something. Negotiations must never be narrowed to just one issue if possible, because with one issue someone generally wins while the other party loses. When someone wins and another loses, there will be bitter feelings and, in the long run, poor results.

Nor should negotiators make the mistake of thinking that the other party wants the same thing that your side does. There is a classic negotiation story often used in training about two young women who each wanted an orange. They fought over the orange until their mother intervened and asked specific questions about why they wanted the orange. It seems that while they both wanted the orange, one wanted the juice to drink while the other wanted the peel for baking. Different people desire different things in life and price is not always the most important consideration.

An effective supervisor must have a working knowledge of negotiation techniques and must use them whenever appropriate to attain desired leadership goals for the organization. While vital in leadership situations, negotiation skills are used effectively in everyday communication as well as in business discourse.

The Three Stages of Negotiation:

1. Determining what the other side wants,

2. Communicating to the other side what you want, and

3. Seeking a compromise so that both sides can accomplish their objectives.

Negotiation Skills

- The ability to gather information. In one sense, those with criminal justice backgrounds have an advantage in that they have been taught to objectively gather facts and evaluate information.

- The ability to negotiate and make decisions without emotion. Of course, your heart may be in your throat through much of the negotiation contact but the learned skill of wearing a poker face and acting as if reaching an agreement were not the most important thing in life at the time gives a negotiator a decided advantage over one whose emotion (anger, delight, gloating or envy) is evident throughout all or part of the process.

- The ability to separate an interest from a position. As has been stated above, a position is what someone describes their desired state or goal to be, while an interest is what their goal really is. An experienced negotiator will, through astute questioning, quickly attempt to determine the true interest of the other party and will seek ways to meet the other party's needs in order that an agreement might be reached.

- The ability to remain silent. Often individuals reach a point in the negotiation where there is a seeming impasse. Rather than continue the conversation for the sake of maintaining appearances, good negotiators understand that if they cease talking, the other side will become extremely uncomfortable and will feel compelled to talk, especially if they believe that the negotiation is about to collapse. Their speech will frequently result in a compromise or offer to give something up in order to maintain the dialogue. Silence, though it cuts against the grain of modern discourse, can be an extremely useful tactic and should be considered throughout any negotiation process.

- The ability to use time. Time is a great ally to one who can use it wisely. Understand in advance what your time pressures are so that you will not be forced into an agreement. Conversely, knowing that both sides are under time pressure should keep a negotiator from feeling intimidated. However, if the other side is under time pressure and you are not, you have a great advantage, especially if they are unaware of your knowledge.

- Knowledge of your BATNA (Best Alternative to a Negotiated Agreement). Good negotiators should always understand their BATNA; that is, they should always enter negotiations understanding their bottom line agreement parameter or authority, the lowest price they will meet, the least they will settle for, or the greatest amount to which they will agree, depending upon the situation. Knowing one's bottom line gives a great advantage in any negotiation, but only if the negotiator remains within the agreed upon parameter. A negotiator who gets caught in the enthusiasm of the negotiation and strays beyond the parameters of the BATNA is not serving the client's best interest, particularly if the negotiator is also the client.

Specific Negotiating Tactics

- Good Guy/Bad Guy. Every law enforcement officer is familiar with this tactic as it is one of the most basic (and yet extremely effective) tactics used in negotiations. It begins with one negotiator acting as if he or she is extremely sympathetic to the other side's plight. At some point the sympathizing negotiator will introduce either directly or by implication the bad guy, usually his or her partner, and make it clear to the other side that it is more advantageous to deal with the sympathizing negotiator than with the partner. Once the hook has been set, the sympathizing negotiator will offer what appears to be the best deal the other side will get, and if the other side does not act quickly, the sympathizing negotiator will not be responsible for the consequences.

    o Law-enforcement officers must be very careful when using this technique so as not to portray the prosecutor as the bad guy who wants to prosecute the subject to the fullest extent possible, because the officer may then be stepping over the line and negotiating with the subject illegally. Only prosecutors are given the authority to plea bargain with subjects and when a law-enforcement officer engages in this activity, it is normally considered illegal and a confession resulting from it may be deemed inadmissible at trial.

- o The counter to a Good Guy/Bad Guy tactic is to advise the other side that you understand the Good Guy/Bad Guy tactic is being used, that it won't work, and that the opponent needs to get serious if the negotiations are to continue. Another counter involves threatening to appeal to the opponent's supervisor because it does not appear that the opponent is negotiating in good faith.

- The Nibble. Many negotiators attempt to nibble after an agreement has been reached. They understand that the opposite party is usually happy with the deal and is therefore vulnerable to the thought of possibly losing an agreement over a small issue. For example, two individuals negotiate the sale of a firearm. After haggling over the price and discussing the age and condition of the firearm, they finally reached an agreement. Almost as an afterthought, the buyer says, "Of course, the sale **does** include that box of bullets." If the seller fails to think quickly, he or she will probably agree to the nibble.

  - o Remember that nibbles are tactics on the part of negotiators to squeeze one last benefit from the other party after the agreement has been reached.

  - o Nibbles are effectively countered by insinuating that the nibbler is cheap: "Come on, you have just bought a great gun for an extremely low price. You don't really expect me to have to pay for your bullets too, do you?"

- The Validity Test. If the opposite party advises that they will not settle for less than $50,000 or they will litigate the issue, a negotiator should always test this figure for validity by asking the party something like, "You mean that if my client is willing to pay a reasonable amount but it is not quite $50,000, you would refuse to discuss the matter?" Testing for validity will determine whether or not an individual is willing to compromise his or her position. If the test shows that they are willing to compromise even a little, this can be taken as a sign that they are generally ready to negotiate the entire issue, despite their original uncompromising position

- The Appeal to Higher Authority. Negotiators frequently have a higher authority to which they must refer before a decision may be made. By appealing to a higher authority a negotiator gains time to consider a proposal through shifting blame to a higher authority, who is normally some vague entity such as a committee (banks always have a loan committee), an attorney, the prosecutor, the warden or the chief.

- o The higher authority often does not even have to be named to be effective. Just saying that the negotiator has no authority to do the thing requested but will seek approval is generally sufficient.

- o The first counter to the appeal to higher authority is to determine from the outset whether or not the other party has agreement making authority. If not, the negotiator may wish to postpone the mediation until clearer decision-making power is obtained.

- o Other counters include asking the other party to agree that if a settlement between the negotiators themselves can be reached, should the deal itself not be concluded at that time? This places time pressure on the other party to reach an agreement and to seek approval of the higher authority at the same time.

- o Hostage negotiators frequently make use of higher authority to delay complying with unreasonable demands.

- o A final counter involves urging the other party to reach an agreement "subject to the approval" of the higher authority.

- Deadlocks and how to break them. Occasionally during a negotiation the parties run into a brick wall where no one will budge. As was stated above, silence can be effectively used in this situation. Another tactic to break a deadlock involves setting aside the deadlocked issue and continuing to negotiate and reach agreement on the remainder of the issues. It is not necessarily important to negotiate the largest issues first and so the negotiation may move from issue to issue. If no agreement can be reached, the proceedings sometimes may be helped by bringing in another negotiator who essentially acts as a neutral mediator to move the process along.

- Tips for Everyday Negotiating.

    - o Never jump at the first offer. The skillful negotiator usually says no even when presented with a reasonable offer. This will ultimately cause the other side to feel that they have reached a good deal and will often get you a better deal.

- Never argue - always agree and gradually turn them around.

- Never act like an expert or act too sophisticated. Sophisticated people invite competition, which is not what you want.

- Anytime you make a concession, ask for a concession on the part of the other side right away.
  - This is the Trade Off Principle: get an early delivery date, etc.
  - "If we do that for you, what can you do for us?"
  - Never give anything away, always ask for something in return.
  - If they know you will do this, it stops them from constantly coming back for more.

- Be Prepared To Walk Away.

  - If you really want the item above all else, you have lost the negotiation before it has begun.

  - Your BATNA must be decided on in advance!

  - You must communicate to the other side that you are prepared to walk away.

- Flinching: Be prepared to flinch at their proposal. If not, they will add on conditions.

  - People are watching for your reaction.

  - It does not have to be theatrical but it must be a visible reaction in order to be effective.

Beware of:

- The Shrinking Offer. When it is obvious that one side is attempting to steamroll a position, the other side uses smaller offers with each contact by deferring to their higher authority for the decision.

- Jumping to draft the contract or agreement. If a contract is involved, the one to write it may place clauses that are favorable to that side. The other side must then negotiate them out of the contract. To keep the other side honest, it is best if you or your attorney (prosecutor) draft the agreement.

- The Fait Accompli, made by sending a contract and a check. This will likely cause the other side to:

    o Accept, or

    o Negotiate the entire contract, or

    o Begin with the contract and negotiate separate parts.

- Red Herrings: False issues to throw away - so be careful only to negotiate the real issue.

- The Puppy Dog Close: "Take the puppy home over the weekend and if you don't like it, bring it back," which they never did. In this ploy, the negotiator gets the other side emotionally involved in the decision. This emphasizes the necessity to portray yourself as an unemotional party even if in reality your position is anything but unemotional.

- Splitting the Difference.

    o One standard negotiation tactic is to never make an offer to "split the difference" first: let the other side do it.

    o When the other side offers to split the difference, the negotiator asks them how much that would be (making the other side name the price), and then delays the decision, appealing to a higher authority. On the next contact, the negotiator advises that the authority won't meet the figure, but the two sides are so close it's a pity to back out of the negotiations. Often the other side will then offer to split the difference again.

    o The rule is never offer to split the difference but encourage other side to do so.

Understanding Power

In every negotiation, you ether feel you are in control or others are in control. You are either the intimidator or intimidated. There are different kinds of power depending upon the person and the position:

- Position Power: Power that comes with the territory, such as Presidents, Corporate CEOs or Organizational Heads.

- Reward or Punishment Power: The perception that this person has the power to either reward or punish (police officers writing tickets have this power).

- Reverent Power: Projecting a consistent set of values (Billy Graham, Ronald Reagan).

- Charismatic Power: Power due to the personality of the person (Bill Clinton).

- Expertise Power: Power coming from perceived expertise of the person (Doctors and Lawyers are good at this). If a negotiator has Reverent Power, Charismatic Power and Expertise Power together, he or she can often control a negotiation.

- Situational Power: Postal employees and governmental employees.

- Information Power: Having information or secrets often gives a person control over a given situation.

If control is being lost during a negotiation, examine the opponent's source of power. Once you understand the source of power, it can be dealt with.

Leaders generally have at least four kinds of power:

- Title Power

- Reward Power

- Reverent Power

- Charismatic Power

These elements of power can be used either for good or bad, as evidenced by the leadership exerted by individuals as diverse as Adolph Hitler, John Kennedy and Ronald Reagan.

The Importance of Information

As a general rule, the side with the most information will do better in the negotiation; in fact, the side with the most information usually controls the negotiation. Henry Kissinger, in talking about the Geneva Arms Talks, answered a question about whether we knew what the Russians were going to propose by saying that we wouldn't have been at the table if we had not known what they were going to propose.

In seeking information, always ask open-ended questions, like why? And how? Also, don't forget to ask how people feel about certain things. People will give an amazing amount of information if the right questions are asked.

Pointers for Seeking Information:

- Ask people who have done business with the other side.

- Ask employees on a lower level than the negotiators - secretaries, engineers, mechanics, etc.

- The location where questions are asked is important: questioners are more likely to get information when the questions are asked in a neutral area such as a restaurant.

- Gathering Information is the second step in the negotiating process (the first step is establishing criteria, the open agenda and the hidden agenda, while the third step is reaching for bold compromises that will accomplish a settlement).

Sources

Brinkman, Rick, and Rick Kirschner. <u>Dealing With People You Can't Stand</u>. New York: McGraw-Hill, 1994.

Cohen, Allan R., and David L. Bradford. <u>Influence Without Authority</u>. New York: John Wiley & Sons, 1990.

Craver, Charles B. <u>Effective Legal Negotiating</u>. Williamsburg, VA: International Communications Corporation, 2001.

Dawson, Roger. <u>Secrets of Power Negotiating</u>. Franklin Lakes, NJ: Career Press, 1995.

Fisher, Roger, and William Ury. <u>Getting to Yes</u>. New York: Penguin Books, 1981.

Nierenberg, Gerald. <u>The Art of Negotiation</u>. New York: Warner Publishing, 1985.

Slaikeu, Karl A. <u>When Push Comes to Shove</u>. San Francisco: Jossey-Bass, 1996.

Supervisory Liability   Chapter 13

"Recognizing that supervisory liability can extend to the highest levels of state government, we have noted that liability ultimately is determined by pinpointing the persons in the decision making chain whose deliberate indifference permitted the constitutional abuses to continue unchecked."

Shaw v. Stroud 115 S.Ct 67 (1994)

Recent Changes in General Liability Exposure

In 1990, more than 18,000,000 civil suits were filed in the United States. This represented a 30 percent increase over the six preceding years. In 1960, there were 260,000 lawyers in the United States; there are over 800,000 today. Three years ago there were eight civil verdicts in which the damage award was over $100 million. One of the largest verdicts was a $5 billion award for wrongful death. The verdict was against a serial killer who subsequently died in prison and so the award was more of a moral victory for the plaintiffs than anything else: however, it follows the general trend of ever increasing damage awards.

Some research studies have shown that there are now more than 77 new legal theories per year providing unique and often bizarre ways to sue for redress of injury. The rise of arbitration cases throughout America has been attributed directly to the phenomenal increase in the number of civil suits over the past 10 years. For example, in the early 1960s there were, in most years, less than 300 federal civil rights suits against law enforcement officers. Today, there are over 33,000 cases per year (with an additional 30,000 cases against corrections personnel). It is interesting that 97 percent of these cases are dismissed before trial, and of those that continue, only 13 percent are ultimately successful. Most are filed claiming that the officer did not have probable cause during an arrest or that excessive force was used even though probable cause may have been present. Additionally, cases are being filed against officers for illegal search and seizure (Fourth Amendment Violation) and even for coerced confessions (Fifth and Sixth Amendment Violations).

Legal Trends

Today, even prosecutors can be held liable for advice that they provide to law enforcement officers *Burns v. Reed*, 111 S.Ct. 1934 (1991).

In Federal Court, officers and other officials generally rely on the Qualified Immunity Defense (Bivens Defense), which states that an officer or official is not liable civilly if the officer had a reasonable, good-faith belief in the legality of his or her actions and if the law claimed to have been violated was not well settled, *Bivens v. Six Unknown Federal Narcotics Agents*, 403 U.S. 388 (1971). Despite this defense, an officer may be held liable even if the officer procured a search or arrest warrant if the officer should have known that probable cause was not present, *Malley v. Briggs*, 475 U.S. 335, L 339 340 (1986).

The Supreme Court in *Hunter v. Bryant*, 112 S.Ct. 534 (1991), ruled that qualified immunity is for a judge to decide, not a jury. The practical effect of this ruling is that if the judge finds that officers made a reasonable mistake and did not have probable cause, but if it were a close question, the judge may dismiss the complaint upon a motion for summary judgment rather than sending the case to a jury. If there is a dispute over the facts, however, the judge has no choice but to send the case to a jury.

This defense does not hold for government entities (except for states and state officials) because good faith is not a defense for a government (city or county). Under the main civil rights statute (Title 18 U.S.C. Section 1983), the plaintiff must show that the government or government officials had a policy or custom which produced a constitutional violation and actual injury. Further, the plaintiff must show that the official's policy or custom was established through "deliberate indifference to citizen's constitutional rights." Note that the policy or custom is often claimed to be improper training or lack of training. This is known as a "deep pockets" theory because if the elements are proven, it does not matter that the officials may have acted in good faith or believed that the actions they took were reasonable and legal under the circumstances.

Examples of cases flowing from this legal theory are:

- Failure to Train: *Harris County, Texas vs. Walsweer*, 50 Cr. L 3021 (S.Ct, 1991). Deputies negligently fired guns while answering a disturbance call and injured a bystander. Section 1983 damages were awarded because the lack of training was well known by county administrators.

- *Davis v. Mason Co.*, 927 F.2d, 1473 (1991), was a case taking failure to train one step further when the Ninth Circuit Court of Appeals held that law enforcement agencies may be held liable for failure to educate officers about the continuing developments in the law.

- In *Russo vs. Massulo*, 50 Cr L 3016, (S.Ct, 1991), the Supreme Court held that an officer leading an arrest party who also lied in an arrest affidavit was not entitled to qualified immunity, but others on the arrest team had qualified immunity because they relied on his statements.

Negligence in Employment Cases

Of course, traditional state law holds a person responsible for negligent or intentional acts, with damage awards being dependent upon the extent of the negligence, severity of the injury, and other contributory factors.

Under the principal that an employer is responsible for the negligent acts of the employee, state courts have historically held employers liable when an employee commits a negligent act within the scope of the employee's responsibility. These actions are separate from negligent actions against the employee and essentially force the employee to be a witness against the employer.

Section 1983 cases have held not only that an official may violate the civil rights of another person through negligent acts, but that a supervisor or administrator may also be held liable if the supervisor's personal negligent conduct essentially caused the employee to engage in a violation of someone's civil rights.

This liability has been applied to the following situations:

- Negligent Employment, occurring where the employee was so inept or dangerous that he or she should never have been hired.

- Negligent Retention, occurring where an obviously unfit employee was not terminated.

- Negligent Assignment, occurring where the supervisor knew or should have known that the employee was obviously unfit for a particular assignment.

- Negligent Entrustment, occurring where the employer should never have provided equipment (firearms, nightsticks, vehicles) for the use of an inept or dangerous employee.

- Failure to Train, occurring where the supervisor or department exhibits "deliberate indifference" to training and this lack of training produced negligent acts resulting in injuries.

- Failure to Supervise, occurring when the supervisor either knew or should have known that the employee's negligence was likely to cause injury. If the supervisor is an "official policy maker," the employing municipal corporation may also be held liable.

- Failure to Direct, occurring where inappropriate policies and procedures have been implemented, resulting in negligent acts and injuries.

Sexual Harassment Claims

There has been a virtual explosion of litigation following the passage of the Civil Rights Act of 1991, particularly in harassment claims. This act allowed plaintiffs to request jury trials and provided for both compensatory and punitive damages. The courts have increasingly widened the theories upon which suits could be brought and have encouraged suits or threatened suits. Recent cases indicate that it is not enough for employers to draft anti-harassment policies and/or investigate internal complaints. Employers must now take a pro-active position toward sexual harassment and must be extremely aggressive in both preventing it before it happens and in stopping it once it has occurred.

The Law

Title VII of the Civil Rights Act of 1964 states that it is *an unlawful employment practice for an employer.., to discriminate against an individual with respect to compensation, terms, conditions, or privileges of employment because of such individual's sex.*

There are four main issues leading to Title VII sexual harassment claims:

- General Harassment. Courts have enlarged the basis for the claim, so that now a gender based harassment can support a sexual harassment claim. This means that harassing, abusive, and crude remarks may constitute sexual harassment even when a supervisor directs remarks to all employees, male and female.

- o The key here is when the supervisor's conduct is so severe that it alters the conditions of employment and creates a hostile, abusive work environment, sexual harassment claims generally will be upheld.

- o Under this theory, male employees may also file claims against female supervisors for sexual harassment.

- Same Sex Harassment. The lower courts were split on the issue of whether or not same-sex harassment could exist. The Supreme Court finally settled this issue in the case of *Oncale v. Sundowner Offshore Services, Inc.*, 523 U.S. 75 (1998), a case in which the victim, a male on an offshore oil rig, was threatened with rape by his supervisor and co-workers, all males.

    - o The Court held that sex discrimination consisting of same-sex sexual harassment is actionable under Title VII. Title VII's prohibition of discrimination "because of … sex" protects men as well as women.

    - o Harassment based on sexual orientation is not actionable at this time under Title VII, which prohibits harassment based on gender, not sexuality. Note that a growing number of states protect sexual orientation under state law.

- Quid Pro Quo Harassment. There are two areas of liability under this provision.

    - o Where unwelcome sexual favors are a condition of employment, or

    - o Where unwelcome sexual favors are sought by threatening or causing a detriment to a job.

    - o Most courts have held strict liability here against supervisors because they are the very entities who are should prevent it.

    - o Recent decisions have held that a threat of economic harm was enough, rather than actual proof of economic harm.

- Hostile Work Environment Harassment. Three Elements must be proved under this provision:

- That the supervisor made
  - Sexual Advances, or
  - Requested Sexual Favors, or
  - Engaged in Physical Conduct of a Sexual Nature.
- That the conduct was unwelcome, and
- That the conduct was severe or pervasive enough to
  - Alter the conditions of the victim's employment, and
  - Create an abusive working environment.
- In determining the existence of a hostile work environment, courts place great emphasis on factors such as
  - Frequency of conduct.
  - Severity of the Discrimination.
  - Presence of physical threats, and
  - Whether the conduct interfered with the victim employee's work performance.
- Isolated or trivial incidents don't usually qualify for hostile work environment, but when management participated in the actions, the employer is automatically liable. Where a co-worker engages in harassment, an employer is liable when the employer authorized, knew or should have known about the harassment, and failed to take prompt and adequate corrective measures. From this it is clear that either actual or constructive knowledge can produce liability.

- Conduct outside the work environment may be actionable at some future time under Title VII; this issue is not settled yet.

Employment Discrimination Claims

There are four major claims which employees may make under Title VII:

- Disparate Treatment: The employer treated the employee or applicant unfavorably because of the employee's membership in a protected class. This claim can be made by individuals or a class (group of people), and the ultimate question is whether the membership in the class was a determining factor in the treatment. The only way to defend against these types of claims is to show solid documentation regarding the employee's substandard performance or qualification.

- Disparate Impact: This is a claim that a neutral policy had an adverse impact on a protected class and that the policy was unnecessary for the effective performance of the job. An example of disparate impact was the often imposed policy in law enforcement that in order to be hired, officers had to be above a certain height (frequently 5 feet, 7 inches). This effectively excluded most female applicants and could not be justified as being necessary for job performance.

- Failure to offer Reasonable Accommodation: The general rule is that employers have an obligation of showing flexibility regarding a person's religious beliefs, practices or disabilities. The employer must make reasonable accommodation unless it would impose an undue hardship on the business. An example would be to acquire or modify equipment, such as wheelchair access.

- Retaliation: It is illegal to retaliate against a complainant. Retaliation damages are allowable even if the original complaint was without merit. Forms of retaliation which are actionable include:

    o Termination.

    o Demotion.

    o Suspension.

    o Isolation.

Employment Discrimination

It is difficult for employers to win these suits consistently when all of the costs are counted. The law is complex and differs from jurisdiction to jurisdiction.

Under Title VII, it is unlawful for an employer to take adverse action against an employee which action is motivated by employee's status as a member of a protected class. Protected Classes are defined by Title VII of Civil Rights Act of 1964 as those based upon:

- Race
- Color
- Religion
- National Origin
- Sex
- Age (The Discrimination in Employment Act of 1967 - 40 years old or older).

Disabilities

The Americans with Disabilities Act (ADA) prohibits discrimination on the basis of disability in the areas of employment, State and local government, public accommodations, commercial facilities, transportation, and telecommunications. It also applies to the United States Congress. Title I of the ADA was passed by Congress in 1990 and became effective on July 26, 1992.

To be protected by the ADA, one must have a disability or have a relationship or association with an individual with a disability. An individual with a disability is defined by the ADA as a person who has a physical or mental impairment that **substantially limits one or more major life activities**, a person who has a history or record of such impairment, or a person who is perceived by others as having such impairment. The ADA does not specifically name all of the impairments that are covered.

Covered Employment Under the ADA

Job discrimination against people with disabilities is illegal if practiced by:

- private employers,

- state and local governments,

- employment agencies,

- labor organizations, and

- labor-management committees.

ADA Title I: Employment

Title I requires employers with 15 or more employees to provide qualified individuals with disabilities an equal opportunity to benefit from the full range of employment-related opportunities available to others. For example, it prohibits discrimination in recruitment, hiring, promotions, training, pay, social activities, and other privileges of employment. It restricts questions that can be asked about an applicant's disability before a job offer is made, and it requires that employers make reasonable accommodation to the known physical or mental limitations of otherwise qualified individuals with disabilities, unless it results in undue hardship. Religious entities with 15 or more employees are covered under title I.

Title I complaints must be filed with the U. S. Equal Employment Opportunity Commission (EEOC) within 180 days of the date of discrimination, or 300 days if the charge is filed with a designated state or local fair employment practice agency. Individuals may file a lawsuit in Federal court only after they receive a "right-to-sue" letter from the EEOC.

ADA Title II: State and Local Government Activities

Title II covers all activities of State and local governments regardless of the government entity's size or receipt of Federal funding. Title II requires that State and local governments give people with disabilities an equal opportunity to benefit from all of their programs, services, and activities (e.g. public education, employment, transportation, recreation, health care, social services, courts, voting, and town meetings).

State and local governments are required to follow specific architectural standards in the new construction and alteration of their buildings. They also must relocate programs or otherwise provide access in inaccessible older buildings, and communicate effectively with people who have hearing, vision, or speech disabilities. Public entities are not required to take actions that would result in undue financial and administrative burdens. They are required to make reasonable modifications to policies, practices, and procedures where necessary to avoid discrimination, unless they can demonstrate that doing so would fundamentally alter the nature of the service, program, or activity being provided.

Covered Employment Practices

The ADA makes it unlawful to discriminate in all employment practices such as:

- Recruitment
- Pay
- Hiring
- Firing
- Promotion
- Job assignments
- Training
- Leave
- Lay-off
- Benefits
- All other employment related activities.

The ADA prohibits an employer from retaliating against an applicant or employee for asserting his or her rights under the ADA

Protected Individuals

Title I of the ADA protects qualified individuals with disabilities from employment discrimination. Under the ADA, a person has a disability if that person has a physical or mental impairment that substantially limits a major life activity. The ADA also protects individuals who have a record of a substantially limiting impairment, and people who are regarded as having a substantially limiting impairment.

- To be protected under the ADA, an individual must have a record of or be regarded as having a substantial, as opposed to a minor, impairment.

- A substantial impairment is one that significantly limits or restricts a major life activity such as hearing, seeing, speaking, breathing, performing manual tasks, walking, caring for oneself, learning or working.

- An individual with a disability must also be qualified to perform the essential functions of the job with or without reasonable accommodation, in order to be protected by the ADA. This means that the applicant or employee must:

    o Satisfy the job requirements for educational background, employment experience, skills, licenses, and any other qualification standards that are job related (employers do not have to lower quality or standards for accommodation); and

    o be able to perform those tasks that are essential to the job, with or without reasonable accommodation.

The ADA does not interfere with the right to hire the best qualified applicant. Nor does the ADA impose any affirmative action obligations. The ADA simply prohibits discriminating against a qualified applicant or employee because of his or her disability.

Essential Functions

Essential functions are the basic job duties that an employee must be able to perform, with or without reasonable accommodation. Employers should carefully examine each job to determine which functions or tasks are essential to performance. (This is particularly important before taking an employment action such as recruiting, advertising, hiring, promoting or firing).
Factors to consider in determining if a function is essential include:

- Whether the reason the position exists is to perform that function,

- The number of other employees available to perform the function, or among whom the performance of the function can be distributed, and

- The degree of expertise or skill required to perform the function.

The employer's judgment as to which functions are essential, and a written job description prepared before advertising or interviewing for a job will be considered by EEOC as evidence of essential functions. Other kinds of evidence that EEOC will consider include:

- The actual work experience of present or past employees in the job,

- The time spent performing a function,

- The consequences of not requiring that an employee perform a function, and

- The terms of a collective bargaining agreement.

The Employer's Obligation to Provide Reasonable Accommodations

EEO guidelines define reasonable accommodation as any change or adjustment to a job or work environment that permits a qualified applicant or employee with a disability to participate in the job application process, to perform the essential functions of a job, or to enjoy benefits and privileges of employment equal to those enjoyed by employees without disabilities. For example, reasonable accommodation may include:

- Acquiring or modifying equipment or devices,

- Job restructuring,

- Part-time or modified work schedules,

- Reassignment to a vacant position,

- Adjusting or modifying examinations, training materials or policies,

- Providing readers and interpreters, and

- Making the workplace readily accessible to and usable by people with disabilities.

Reasonable accommodation also must be made to enable an individual with a disability to participate in the application process and to enjoy benefits and privileges of employment equal to those available to other employees.

It is a violation of the ADA to fail to provide reasonable accommodation to the known physical or mental limitations of a qualified individual with a disability, unless to do so would impose an undue hardship on the operation of your business. Undue hardship means that the accommodation would require significant difficulty or expense.

Requiring Medical Examinations or Asking Questions about an Individual's Disability

It is unlawful under the ADA to ask an applicant whether he or she is disabled or about the nature or severity of a disability. It is even unlawful to require the applicant to take a medical examination before making a job offer.

After a job offer is made, however, and prior to the commencement of employment duties, it may be required that an applicant take a medical examination if everyone who will be working in the job category must also take the examination. The job offer may be conditioned on the results of the medical examination.

Applicants may be asked questions about ability to perform job-related functions, as long as the questions are not phrased in terms of a disability. Applicants may be asked to describe or to demonstrate how, with or without reasonable accommodation; the applicant will perform job-related functions.

Use of Illegal Drugs and Protection under the ADA

The ADA protects HIV, drug or alcohol addiction if the person can perform the essential function of employment with or without reasonable accommodation.

Anyone who is currently using drugs illegally is not protected by the ADA and may be denied employment or fired on the basis of such use. The ADA does not prevent employers from testing applicants or employees for current illegal drug use, or from making employment decisions based on verifiable results. A test for the illegal use of drugs is not considered a medical examination under the ADA; therefore, it is not a prohibited pre-employment medical examination and employees do not have to show that the administration of the test is job related and consistent with business necessity. The ADA does not encourage, authorize or prohibit drug tests.

Enforcement and Available Remedies

The provisions of the ADA which prohibit job discrimination will be enforced by the U.S. Equal Employment Opportunity Commission. Employees who believe they have been discriminated against on the basis of their disability may file a charge with the Commission at any of its offices located throughout the United States. A charge of discrimination must be filed within 180 days of the discriminatory act, unless there is a state or local law that also provides relief for discrimination on the basis of disability. In those cases, the complainant has 300 days to file a charge.
The Commission will investigate and initially attempt to resolve the charge through conciliation, following the same procedures used to handle charges of discrimination filed under Title VII of the Civil Rights Act of 1964. The ADA also incorporates the remedies contained in Title VII. These remedies include hiring, promotion, reinstatement, back pay, and attorneys fees. Reasonable accommodation is also available as a remedy under the ADA.

Under the ADA, an employer cannot discriminate with respect to compensation, conditions or privileges of employment. Some state statutes also include sexual orientation as a protected class, but the ADA does not include sexual orientation at the present time.

Jurisdictional Limits

With the exception of state and municipal governments who are covered regardless of size, Title VII and the ADA do not apply unless there are at least 15 employees in the organization. For age discrimination there must be at least 20 employees.

Damages

Damages against employers who have been found in violation of Title VII or ADA provisions include:

- Back Pay.

- Reinstatement to a lost position.

- Attorney's fees.

- Double Damages (called Liquidated Damages) if the employer's violation was found by a jury to be willful.

- Damages for emotional distress.

- Separate punitive damages

Minimizing Liability

Employers, whether in private industry or government service, can take positive steps recognized by the courts to minimize exposure to liability. Among the action steps they may take are:

- Set Expectations: Write and maintain a well thought out and written anti-sexual harassment policy.

- Broadcast Expectations: Let every employee know what is expected through training and information.

- Establish mandatory reporting procedures and insure they are followed. The procedures must:

    o Allow for bypassing the immediate supervisor.

    o Be independent of the normal chain of command.

- Investigate Complaints Promptly,

    o By a qualified individual, and

    o By instituting a thorough investigation

- Conduct anti-sexual harassment training, to include:

    o A discussion of policy, including examples of illegal behavior, and a discussion of procedures for the filing and handling of complaints.

    o Providing ongoing, meaningful training.

- Stay Current in the Field: The law is changing constantly, particularly in this field.

- Avoiding pitfalls in applicant interviews: Interviews must be limited to job-related subjects. The general test for subject matter is whether the information requested is necessary to judge the applicant's competence or job qualifications. There must be no questions about:

    o Marital status.

    o Family status.

    o Family planning decisions.

    o Child care arrangements.

    o Emergency contacts.

    o Religion or religious practices.

- o Parent's national origin.

- o Disability.

- o Language ability (unless necessary for the job).

- o Permissible Question: After describing the job (days, hours, duties), employers can ask whether the applicant can perform the job.

- Employers should:

    - o Establish and use a probationary period for all new employees. A probationary employee may be fired during this period if the employee simply cannot perform the job satisfactorily. Employees are less likely to sue if fired during a probationary period.

    - o Maintain and use a comprehensive employee handbook or policy manual.

        - Employees (and juries) prefer manuals that outline key processes affecting employees.

        - Be careful in drafting a handbook or manual (seek expert assistance).

    - o Conduct and document regular performance reviews. Reviews are extremely important and will be one of the first things requested by an employee's attorney when a suit is filed.

    - o Use severance agreements selectively. Severance agreements typically terminate employment for a consideration (usually a monetary consideration).

    - o Consider the possibility of using insurance to cover employment practices. Policies cover the costs of claims and lawsuits alleging discrimination, but may not be available to governmental agencies.

Finally, employers should understand that preventing employment suits is quicker, fairer and certainly less expensive than defending them. For this reason, employers should consider implementing an Alternative Dispute Resolution system as described in Chapter Eleven. In organizations where these have been instituted, suit numbers have dropped significantly and employers have found that employees are more productive if they understand that complaints will be handled quickly, informally and fairly.

Sources

Alexander Hamilton Institute. The Complete Compliance Guide to Federal Employment Law. Ramsey, NJ: AHI, 2001.

Alexander Hamilton Institute. The Complete Policy Handbook. Ramsey, NJ: AHI, 2001.

Avery, Michael, *et al*. Police Misconduct. St. Paul, MN: West Group, 2001.

Barrineau, H. E. III. Civil Liability in Criminal Justice. Cincinnati, OH: Anderson Publishing, 1994.

Kappeler, Victor E. Critical Issues in Police Civil Liability. Prospect Heights, IL: Waveland Press, 1997.

Meeting Strategies and Networking — Chapter 14

Visits always give pleasure – if not the arrival, the departure.   Portuguese proverb

This chapter will examine meeting basics and perhaps the most important topic discussed in this book from the perspective of career advancement: Networking.

Strategies for Meetings

For people employed in small organizations, meeting strategies probably makes no sense. Why would you have a class or listen to a lecture on how to run a meeting? Don't you just call people together and talk when the situation calls for it? Do you really need an agenda? Isn't a group meeting ordinarily conducted in every organization on a daily basis, and is this not the best way to handle an employee meeting?

Admittedly the ideas presented here work best in large organizations where a more formalized meeting culture exists, but even in small organizations there is much to be learned from this text which could help to organize and run meetings more efficiently. Examine the way meetings are conducted in your own organization. Are they run efficiently and economically? If not, perhaps you should learn a few of the recommendations outlined below and incorporate them into your own organization's meeting culture.

When Should a Meeting Occur?

Meetings should be held only when it is the best way to meet your objective. Routine, daily meeting are often tedious and can be extreme time wasters. Only when a meeting is the best use of organizational time and when there are no viable alternatives available should a meeting be held. Viable alternatives which should be considered include memos, telephone contacts, personal contacts or e-mail.

Who Should Participate?

Only those who can help achieve the objective should attend. The answers to the following questions will help determine the identities of those who can help achieve the objective:

- Who absolutely must be invited (stakeholders and decision makers)?

- Who has the power to answer the questions that will be posed at the meeting?

- Which individuals will support or oppose the objectives, and which will likely be neutral?

- Which individuals are likely to cause trouble if they are not invited?

How Many Should be Invited?

Number of people invited is usually <u>directly proportional</u> to the length of the meeting; in other words, the larger the group, the longer the meeting. The moral to this is that the smallest number possible to accomplish the objective should be invited.

Meeting Preparation

In order to be efficient, the meeting organizer should always send a memo or agenda to the likely participants. This memo will alert the participants as to the subject and will enable them to arrive prepared to discuss the listed topics. The memo should include the following items:

- A statement of the subject matter or topic.

- Beginning and ending times.

- Location of the meeting.

- Meeting participants.

- Preparation expected of the participants.

Organizer's Groundwork

The organizer should clearly understand the objective prior to calling a meeting. The objectives of supporters, opponents and key people should also be understood, if possible.

Conducting the Meeting

The leader should always be placed in the most visible position, which is usually the farthest away from the entrance. Participants should note that their best position would be opposite the leader.

The leader must begin with an opening statement which is rehearsed but not read. Other elements of a successful meeting are:

- Staying within the allotted time.

- Proper presentation.

    o Visual aids are useful if not overdone.

    o Aids and handouts are meant to be seen, not read during the meeting. Although it is difficult to do, most presentation experts advise that handouts are more effective if distributed at the end of a meeting rather than during a meeting in order to prevent participants from reading through the material, thus losing their concentration on the speaker. A compromise may be made here in which the outline is distributed at the meeting and detailed handouts are available at the conclusion.

- Subject control. The leader must be careful to move the discussion along when participants begin to wander to other topics. This must be done with tact, however, in order not to anger and thus lose support of those who participate primarily to hear themselves speak or those who wish to move to their own agendas.

- Latecomers. For decision makers, it is often best to wait for their arrival. For others, especially those who are not vitally important to the success of the meeting, it is best to begin without them. Some companies even lock the doors of the meeting place a few minutes after the meeting has begun in order to prevent latecomers from disrupting the ongoing meeting.

Networking

If you think about everyone you have ever met, everyone in your family, your friends, schoolmates, church and association members, business contacts, teachers, coaches, neighbors and everyone else you know, you will have a list of hundreds of names. If you diligently compiled those names and indexed them by location, occupation and area of influence, you would have an incredible list - a list that could be commercially marketable, but which is worth much more to you personally in an effort to obtain employment initially and to advance in that employment later.

The reader may think that this is a crass exploitation of friendship, but the basic fact is that the vast majority of employment positions and promotions are obtained through networking rather than through blind applications, resumes or contacts. Because of this, politicians, including George Bush (the elder) and Bill Clinton, are known for making extensive use of their contacts. George Bush was even dubbed "the Rolodex Kid" by the news media. Prior to becoming President, Bill Clinton was said to have entered in his Rolodex at the end of the day the names of every person he met, along with some descriptive data or personal story about them. Imagine the surprise a person would experience upon receiving a birthday card from such a well-known figure, along with some comment about the person's family. It is no secret how politicians such as these are elected to office. The secret is hard work, and a personal database.

Politicians are not the only individuals, however, who can and should keep personal databases. Many studies have shown that people generally do not care how much you know about them once they find out that you care about them. Many companies (law enforcement included) keep detailed files on their contacts, including every detail they can glean.

If you start today writing down names and information about fellow students and business associates, you will probably collect 300 to 600 names and contacts in the next five years. Why should you do this? If you cannot answer the question, "Do you know where your next job, promotion or position will take you, or even what you will be doing ten years from now?" with any certainty, then you need to start keeping a contact list immediately.

The following items should be included in a contact list (remember, the little things mean everything):

- Name, including nickname, spelled correctly.

- Name of spouse and children.

- Hobbies and interests.

- Birthdays.

- Employment, including company name, position and job description.

It is essential to understand that this is not done simply to establish an advantage over other people or to use people for personal gain. Although keeping a contact list will definitely help a career, the main reason that one should be kept is to help other people in their careers and in their personal lives. Most senior executives in large companies attribute their success to others helping them, and in large organizations it is expected that supervisors, no matter what their rank in the organization, will assist the careers of the employees under them.

While it is possible to keep an excellent contact list in a 3 by 5 card box, a Rolodex offers a much better method that affords easier access and is generally expandable as the list increases. Recently, however, advances in computer software have made available programs designed specifically for managing contacts. Programs such as ACT, Sharkware and Info Select have revolutionized contact lists and greatly expanded their capabilities. It is not necessary to use a specific contact list software program, as any database or spreadsheet program can be adapted as a contact list. One recently reviewed program is Evernote, a freeform database that globally indexes every word or item in the database. A great advantage of this program is that it is free. It may be obtained through www.evernote.com.

One of the newest additions to both time management and contact list technologies has been the introduction of the Palm Pilot and similar devices, commonly called personal digital assistants (PDAs) and their offspring, smartphones like the Blackberry, IPhone and Android. With miniaturized circuitry and software programs, the PDA/smartphone market has exploded in the last five years. These devices, most of which are not much larger than a deck of cards, can hold incredible amounts of information, and actually run hundreds of programs.

Using the System to Obtain Jobs and Promotions

The United States Bureau of Labor Statistics, which actually keeps all sorts of detailed and sometimes obtuse data, advises that:

- 70 percent of all jobs are found through networking.

- Only two percent are found through sending out resumes.

- 10 to 15 percent are found through classified ads, and

- Four percent were self-created.

From these statistics it is obvious that the best way to get a job, as well as to get promoted, is to rely on a networking association, including friends, family and business associates. This would include associates both ahead and behind you on the departmental ladder. Another avenue is through occupational associations. Joining one or more of these associations increases exposure to others in your field and widens your contact list beyond the immediate geographical boundaries of your employment. There are, fortunately, a number of existing organizational associations in the criminal justice field, with most charging only a modest amount for membership.

Associations and friendships, as vital as they are, will not guarantee that you will keep a job once you have obtained it. For that guarantee, you will need to place into practice what you have learned from this and other works. You should never stop striving for improvement, both in your personal life and in your career field. This book is a road map pointing you toward career success. It is built upon a lifetime of experience and the work of numerous experts in both corporate and government fields. The bottom line, however, is up to you. Learning the principles is the first step, applying and refining them is the second, and following through with your network is the third and final step of your career journey.

Sources

Frank, Milo. <u>How to Run a Successful Meeting in Half the Time</u>. New York: Simon and Schuster, 1981.

Frank, Milo. <u>How to Get Your Point Across in 30 Seconds or Less</u>. New York: Simon and Schuster, 1981.

MacKay, Harvey. <u>How to Build a Network of Power Relations</u>. Niles, IL: Nightingale-Conant, 1995.

Media Relations Chapter 15

If you want to survive in the Bureau, stay away from the media. If asked a question by a reporter, the last thing you want to say is, "No comment."   H. Edward McNulty, FBI Special Agent, Seattle, Washington 1970

Introduction

In a few sentences, describe your worst experience in dealing with the media:

_____

_____

_____

_____

Criminal justice personnel and media representatives have often experienced a confrontational and adversarial relationship. CJ personnel often criticize the Media for focusing on the negative aspects of their work, while claiming that the Media overlooks many of their good activities that they should be exposed to the public.

In your opinion does the news media use bias and prejudice in reporting incidents about your organization? If so, why?

_____

_____

James Madison wrote: "A popular Government without popular information or the means of acquiring it is but a prologue to a farce or a tragedy or perhaps both. Knowledge will forever govern ignorance, and a people who mean to be their own Governors must arm themselves with the power knowledge gives."

The U.S. Constitution states, "Congress shall make no Law…abridging the Freedom of Speech, or of the press."

The Role of Media

The role of the news services of a community is to get the news and inform the public. These services perform two functions in the criminal justice system's relationship with the public: 1) it allows citizens to make informed choices rather than acting out of ignorance; and, 2) it serves as a "report card" by ensuring criminal justice organizations are upholding their professional standards and conforming to the "will of the people" as expressed in laws of the land.

The Role of Government Service

Criminal justice organizations provide many services to the public which it serves. Most of these services are dictated by laws and ordinances. It becomes the duty of each organization's leadership to ensure that they are carrying out their assigned tasks in an efficient, effective and economical manner with a high degree of professionalism. They must also recognize the right of the public to be fully and accurately informed in all matters of public interest. In order to achieve these goals they must maintain a relationship with members of the media that is based upon trust, cooperation, and mutual interest.

Purpose of the FOIA

Historically, the Media and ordinary citizens had to prove they had a right to gain access to official governmental records. However, in 1966 the *Freedom of Information Act*

(Title 5, U.S. Code, Section 522) was passed and placed the burden on the government to prove that people did not have the right to know certain information.

The overriding purpose of the original FOIA and its subsequent changes was summarized in a 1993 report to the U. S. House of Representatives."The Freedom of Information Act (FOIA) establishes a presumption that records in the possession of agencies and departments of the executive branch of the U.S. Government is accessible to the people…with the passage of the FOIA the burden of proof shifted from the individual to the government."

The FOIA does provide some limited exceptions which exempt full disclosure of nine specific types of information, including records relating to:

National defense of Foreign policy

Trade secrets

Matters involving criminal investigations

Suggestions for Good Media Relations

Most of the following suggestions for establishing and maintaining good relations with the media are common sense. They also encompass basic communications protocol and proper methods of ensuring that misunderstandings do not occur.

- Be friendly and polite no matter how traumatic the situation.

- Be as helpful as your organizational guidelines allow.

- Cooperation is a two-way street.

- Make sure every detail (names, facts, figures) is accurate. Proof and reproof your release.

- Try to be prompt with releases. Old news is no news.

- State the facts of the matter without exaggeration.

- Be truthful – if you don't know or cannot respond to a question, say so.

- Include all significant facts as possible.

- Treat all media representatives alike. Do not show favoritism.

- Accept the fact that building good media relationships take time.

Suggestions for Practices to Avoid

- Never lie.

- Never threaten or demand.

- Do not lose your temper.

- Do not overstate the importance of your information.

- Avoid giving your opinion – just state the facts.

- Accept at least partial responsibility for nonfactual information reported by the media and attributed to you.

- Understand that reporters have rules and regulations to follow just like you.

- Do not speak "off the record." Eventually you will be betrayed.

Written Press Releases

Almost any editor of a newspaper or news director of a television station prefers to have a manuscript or document about a situation that an organization wishes to have printed or broadcast to the public. This serves to eliminate communication errors that may occur over the telephone.

The written format of a press release may vary but should conform to the following guidelines.

- The news release should always be typewritten.

- Use spell and grammar check.
- Get another person to read the document for clarity before it is disseminated.
- Use the agency's letterhead stationary should be used if available.
- Do not exceed two type-written pages.
- Double space the press release and print it on only one side of the paper.

Press Release Dissemination

Getting the press release out to media representatives in a timely fashion is essential to a good working relationship. A Fax or e-mail is commonly used to promptly contact all media outlets. Other mediums include providing a printed copy to each outlet by courier or by telephonic transmission. The press release should contain the date and time of the release and the "point of contact" for your organization. Keep a dissemination record in your file for future reference.

The structure of a press release is the inverted pyramid. It simply means that you should put the most important or enticing information in the first few sentences of your press release, and then unfold the rest of the story in descending order of importance.

Answering Questions Effectively

- Anticipate and prepare for questions ahead of time
- Analyze the audience
- Actively listen to questions
- Repeat the question
- Define terms

- Divide multiple questions
- Be brief and to the point
- Support opinions with evidence
- Avoid arguments
- Admit when you don't know
- Avoid the original questioner
- Involve the entire audience
- Don't let questioners give speeches
- Reward certain questions

Guidelines to Ending the Question-and-Answer Period

Media conferences are usually scheduled to begin at a specific time. However, there is usually no set time for it to conclude. Here are some guidelines to consider when bringing the conference to an end:

- When questions from the media do not relate to reason that the press conference was called
- When questions begin to address matters which cannot be discussed
- When reporters continually repeat the same question in hopes of eliciting an answer due to their persistence
- When questions are not readily forthcoming

More Tips for Media Success

- Project sincerity and credibility
- Be nice, responsive, and careful
- Remember that you always are on the record – all of the time
- Keep it simple and stay on point
- Look at the reporters, not the cameras
- Remember that appearance and body language are important
- Understand the reporter's question before you answer
- Avoid "shop talk" and speak clearly
- Refrain from using the word "I" if possible
- Leave the media with an effective quote that will sum up your position and serve as a usable sound bite
- Be ready to think on the spur of the moment

"Say it Right"

- Say your piece in 12 seconds or less
- Tell the truth
- Don't use jargon
- Speak on an 8th grade level
- Be friendly and kind
- Confident appearance is essential

Sources

Bennett, W.W. and Karen Hess. *Management and Supervision in Law Enforcement*, 3rd ed. Wadsworth, Belmont, CA., 2001

Brannan, Leigh. *Say it Right*. Presentation at Faulkner University. August, 2007.

Sewell, James D. *Working with the Media in Times of Crisis*. Law Enforcement Bulletin, March 2007.

Working with the Media. Youth in Action Bulletin, March 2000.

The Future   Chapter 16

Those who cannot remember the past are condemned to repeat it.   George Santayana, 20th Century American philosopher and poet.

In this final chapter the authors will provide some estimates of the future of first line supervision based on their past experiences and discussions about the future with present day CJ practitioners. The purpose of this chapter is to stimulate thought among students who are currently CJ practitioners, particularly those who expect to work in their field another 20-plus years. The adage, forewarned is forearmed, applies to the future of management since a number of factors may radically change the manner in which supervisors and subordinates presently interact.

Recruitment and Selection

Gone are the days when criminal justice jobs can be advertised by word of mouth. Laws require extensive announcements to enable all qualified and interested candidates equal opportunity to apply. In some jurisdictions ads are generated and managed by governmental departments at the federal, state and local levels. As finding qualified applicants becomes more challenging, first line supervisors will be called upon to assist in the process by updating job descriptions, speaking to interested groups, and participating in the selection process. (Church 2007)

Technology

The greatest impact on supervision may be the continued but more rapid integration of computer technology in the CJ workplace. Thirty years ago few CJ agencies had a single computer but today even the smallest police departments have at least computer access to criminal information. How the supervisor will use computer technology to manage his or her area of responsibility remains uncertain but certain predictions can be made:

1. To the extent that the supervisor is computer literate, he/she will devise ways to manage personal workloads and to monitor the activities/accomplishments of their subordinates.

2. When provided with computer access and training, the 21st Century supervisor will be able to spend less time on the traditional paper reports and more time devising ways to increase productivity of his/her unit.

3. When given the opportunity to gain computer training, supervisors will jump at the chance to become more computer literate.

4. If the supervisor's CJ agency is not keeping up with similar agencies, the progressive supervisor will independently obtain computer training and implement, as much as the agency will allow, supervisory oversight to improve efficiency.

5. The supervisor's span of control may increase as technology provides a single supervisor the ability to oversee dozens of employees without compromising the quality of supervision.

Training and Education

As rapid discoveries are made in scientific aids and more productive methods are adopted by the business world, training of criminal justice professionals will become essential to job security rather than necessary for promotion. In-service training opportunities will continue to increase both at the federal, state, and local levels. Some on-the-job (OJT) training will still be necessary but will not satisfy the need for productive employees who are needed to "hit the street running" due to the massive amount of work facing criminal justice agencies.

The need for a college-based, liberal arts education will increase as the criminal justice field continues to become more sensitive to diversity and legal issues. In some instances police departments and corrections facilities will begin requiring at least a two-year college degree in order to justify high pay and upgrade job positions. Without significant upgrading of pay and benefits, many criminal justice agencies will be unable to recruit significant numbers of applicants to maintain a workforce. For the supervisor, this means more education to keep up with contemporaries and to advance.

Management Styles

As the criminal justice workforce becomes more educated with increasing higher professional standards, the entry-level employee will need a more participative rather than authoritative management approach. Supervisors will be able to delegate more complex jobs to subordinates as they enter the job with more knowledge, skills and ability. For example, the traditional approach of supervisors in law enforcement agencies has been primarily authoritative based on the para-military nature of their organizations. While the military influence will continue to play a significant role in the training phase and chain of command communications structure, first line supervisors will exercise less control and oversight over their charges.

Conclusion

Recognizing the expertise and professionalism of students or practitioners reading this book, the authors opine that the readers may have a better futuristic view of changes in their particular part of the criminal justice system than many academics and government planners. With that in mind, consider the following questions:

During the next ten years, what changes do you anticipate in your segment of the criminal justice field?

1. _____
2. _____
3. _____
4. _____

What changes do you anticipate in the overall field of criminal justice?

1. _____
2. _____
3. _____
4. _____

Sources

Bennett, Wayne and Karen Hess. (2007). *Management and Supervision in Law Enforcement.* Thompson: Belmont, CA.

Church, Jeffrey. (2007). *Future Trends in Law Enforcement Recruiting.* Online at http://www.officer.com/web/online/Careers-and-Recruitment/Future-Trends-in-Law- Enforcement-Recruiting/12$34918. Access August 31, 2010.

Made in the USA
San Bernardino, CA
13 January 2016